P9-CNH-691

APACHE LIGHTNING

APACHE LIGHTNING

The Last Great Battles of the Ojo Calientes

JOSEPH A. STOUT, JR.

New York
OXFORD UNIVERSITY PRESS
1974

Copyright © 1974 by Oxford University Press
Library of Congress Catalogue Card Number: 74-79635

Printed in the United States of America

For
Carolyn and Sherilyn

PREFACE

The Victorio Campaign of 1877–80 was not the result of an accidental encounter between Americans and Indians. Neither did it unfold in isolation. It was the culmination of three decades of intense conflict between the competing and antagonistic cultures of Indians, Americans, and Mexicans.

Into this one campaign, very diverse frustrations contributed their poison. The conflict was made more difficult of solution by the seething cauldron of civil war in Mexico at this time and by the treachery encouraged by the Mexican scalp bounty system. On the American side, the low priority assigned by the Federal Government to Indian problems, squabbles between American Indian Agents and Army officers for control of the Indians' destiny, and a general inability on the part of whites to treat as legitimate the alien rationale of the Indian lifestyle helped make peaceful solution practically impossible. Indirectly introducing bitterness were the racial hatreds between blacks and whites within the United States Army and the lot of American troops in general—their low pay and status, their long hours, their haughty and self-serving officers and their often cruel punishments. This one campaign is, in fact, a case study of individuals in conflict and of how the complexity of human conflict is compounded by the introduction of race.

Such were the elements of this confrontation. Some people see it as a battle between total good and total evil, while others as one that might have ended more quickly and with less bloodshed. Some apologists for the Indians have called them nature's noblemen fighting to retain their independence, their freedom, their way of life—in short, fighting to preserve those very rights Americans claim to hold dear. Other Americans, more in tune with the attitude of the frontiersman, hold that the Indian was ruthless by nature, savage in society, and an impediment to civilization—one who had to be penned up and forced to abandon his tribal heritage.

The origins of the Victorio campaign were not one-dimensional. There was good and right on both sides, just as there was wrong and evil. Soldiers and Indians, civilians and bureaucrats, were merely human, subject to the same passions, hatreds, and prejudices as are all humans. Indians, Mexicans, and Americans saw themselves fulfilling a special destiny, trying to keep faith with their own ancestors by following a philosophy centuries in the making. Unfortunately, the fulfillment of the dreams of any of these three cultures threatened the others; war was the result.

The Victorio campaign was also part of the conflict between Indian and white that had begun 250 years earlier at Plymouth and Jamestown, of that between white and black that had not been resolved by the Civil War and Reconstruction. Equally, it became a part of a conflict between the United States and Mexico that had been intensified by the war between the two; between American and American, as men vied for economic, social, and political power; and between Mexican and Mexican as revolution and counterrevolution swept the nation. Given these swirling currents and cross-currents of men and cultures in conflict, the wonder is not that one side finally won, but rather that before, during, and after the Victorio campaign ordinary life continued in an unbroken pattern. The optimist will see in this the enduring human spirit, while the pessimist will weep at the cruelty of man seeking to rule his fellowman.

In regard to the description of these Indians as the Ojo Caliente, one more thing must be said. The Apaches of the Southwest were splintered into a dozen and more small bands, each with its own leaders. The Americans and Mexicans who pioneered the region fell into the habit of designating particular groups of these Indians by the region in which they lived; thus there were the White Mountain Apaches, the Pinal Apaches, the Chiricahua Apaches, the Jicarilla Apaches, the Mescalero Apaches, and several others. However, these groups moved about in their pursuit of food and water, and at the new location would be given yet another name. Such was the case with the Apaches led by Victorio, who in fact were the eastern branch of the Chiricahua Apaches of southeastern Arizona. They were known at one time or another as the Gila Apaches, the Gilenos, the Mimbres, the Mimbreños, the Coppermine Apaches, and the Ojo Caliente Apaches (which, when translated into English, gave them yet another name, the Warm Springs Apaches). For reasons of consistency I have chosen in this work to refer to them as the Ojo Caliente, for this was the name applied to them in the late 1870's by the soldiers and civilians in the area.

In writing this book I have incurred numerous debts. Heather M. Loyd, Vicki Withers, and others at the Oklahoma State University Library ferreted out obscure documents that shed light on the story. Jack D. Haley, of the Western History Collection at the University of Oklahoma Library, Charles McClure at the University of Texas El Paso Library, staff members of the University of New Mexico Library and the Western New Mexico University Library, and officials in the Municipal Archive of Chihuahua, Mexico, provided necessary assistance.

I also wish to express deep appreciation for the constant encouragement and help given by Odie B. Faulk, Head of the Department of History at Oklahoma State University. Finally, I thank the editors of Oxford University Press, especially Sheldon Meyer, for patience and help with this manuscript.

Stillwater, Okla.   J. A. S., Jr.
January 1, 1974

CONTENTS

I. THE APACHE HERITAGE 3

II. A CLASH OF CULTURES 21

III. THE INDIAN-FIGHTING ARMY 51

IV. THE FIRST OUTBREAK 75

V. CIVILIANS, RANGERS, AND MEXICANS 111

VI. ARMY ATTEMPTS AT SOLUTION 134

VII. THE FINAL CAMPAIGN 158

CONCLUSION 180

NOTES 184

BIBLIOGRAPHY 195

INDEX 201

APACHE LIGHTNING

1
THE APACHE HERITAGE

Darkness comes slowly to the jagged countryside of the Mimbres Mountains. Shadows cast by jutting peaks lie across the mountain valleys, and the evening sky, first pink, then red, blushes until the last of the sun's rays have departed. Here and there cacti and scrub dot the desert terrain, and deep arroyos lined with water marks from flash floods of years and centuries past scar the landscape. The land is hostile and dangerous. Rattlesnakes and scorpions move silently, and as twilight drifts slowly into darkness only the wind, moaning its way through the vegetation, is heard.

Suddenly, bouncing off canyon walls until it seems to be coming from every direction, a child's desperate cry for his mother bursts into the night. At the foothills of the mountains a form emerges, an old Indian woman gliding through the shadows. Then, almost silently, as if moving on moccasins of air, the only sound a faint rustling, other Indians come out, and the area comes alive with Apaches. Twilight has given way to darkness, giving the Apaches safety from the pursuing United States Army, and these redmen of the Southwest reorganize, searching in the semi-dark of nightfall for families and belongings. For the past twenty hours they have run and crawled across the desert and valleys, finally reaching the foothills of the Mimbres. Trapped against their towering peaks, they have hidden, standing, sitting, crouching nearly motionless for five hours, until now the darkness shields them. Tired, hungry, and thirsty, they at last collapse into deep sleep.

Once again these warriors of the West have escaped the iron jaws of their enemy, this time the hated bluecoats of the United States Cavalry. They are the followers of Victorio, leader of the Ojo Caliente (Warm Springs) Apaches. Doubtless they take little joy in knowing that this incident in the year 1879 is like others common to their ancestors—that the scene is, in fact, one that has occurred many times in the long history of raiding, destruction, and death that is their tribal history and heritage. For 300 years and more, the Apaches of the Southwest have been fighting; sometimes as hunters, other times as hunted, but always in combat, their lives a round of pursuit, capture, and humiliation.

Arriving in the Southwest sometime between A.D. 900 and 1200, the Ojo Caliente Apaches were part of a larger group, known by linguists as Athapascans, who roamed between Mexico and Kansas and from central Texas to western Arizona. They waged war with the earlier inhabitants of the land, and victorious, secured a piece of the territory. However, the desert nature of the terrain had made subdivision of the tribe necessary, and each fragment had developed its own chief, its own identity. The Ojo Caliente Apaches developed an economy and a political-social system based on raiding that kept them at war with their neighbors for centuries. In the 1500's new visitors came, the Spaniards. At first came only transients, seeking golden civilizations to conquer, then in 1598, settlers, ultimately building their villages, plowing their farms, and fencing their ranches in the Rio Grande Valley, as well as in Texas and Arizona. The Apaches were a constant threat to Spanish frontiersmen, to the Mexicans who eventually supplanted the Spanish settlers in 1821, to the Americans who defeated the Mexicans in 1848. Yet neither the *soldados de cuero* carrying the flag of Spain nor the Mexican militiamen marching under the "Eagle and Serpent" were able to subdue the fierce Apaches—and the Americans bearing their "Stars and Stripes" would fail many times before the Indians' end would come.

The tribal way of life had brought out the best—and the worst— in the Apaches. Nomadic in nature, they hated to be confined even briefly. Over the centuries of warring with one tribe or another, they had become so inured to hardship that they seemed to others almost super-human in their ability to withstand pain. They considered themselves "the people," by which they meant that all non-Apaches were something less than human. Thus, while sensitive to the sufferings of their fellow tribesmen, they were not capable of sympathy for outsiders. They saw all non-tribesmen merely as enemies upon whom to inflict torture, slavery, and death. Although by white standards they were uncivilized and brutal, they were most considerate of their own children, whom they treated as their most valuable asset, and they were even ready to adopt the children of their beaten enemies and to extend full tribal membership to them. Being a member of the tribe was a matter of acculturation, not of birth, and an enemy captured as a young lad and raised as an Apache could aspire to and achieve the rank of chief.

From 1540, when the Spaniards first encountered Apaches, these tribesmen were considered the "bad men" of the Southwest. Raiding, stealing silently along trails that seemed to vanish, attacking without warning—even small groups of them were able to intimidate entire armies and large villages. Because of their physical strength, their warlike nature, and their excellent leadership, they were indeed formidable.

From the beginning of Spanish settlement in the Southwest, the Apaches pressured the newcomers. Attacks became so frequent and safety so precarious that as early as 1689 Spanish authorities were calling for an all-out campaign against them. For years thereafter the Spaniards actively sought to convince the hostiles that there was no future in killing travelers or in harassing settlements. Many Apaches were killed and their villages were raided and destroyed, but the ever-moving Indians always retaliated fiercely, exacting a terrible toll in lives and property.

Finally, during the mid eighteenth century, some Apaches agreed to an alliance with the Spaniards against the Comanches—natural enemies of the Apaches. For a short time missions were established in Apache territory in Texas and in other sections of the Southwest. But Spanish efforts to situate Apaches permanently around missions proved ineffective. As soon as the Comanche threat disappeared, the Apaches returned to their former pattern of raiding. The hostiles continued to ravage the frontier, and even the *"compañias volantes,"* the cavalry companies of fast riders taught to chase and fight using Indian strategy, were unable to pursue the Indians into their traditional strongholds. Most of the time the Spaniards could not even find the illusive warriors. In 1767 the Spanish abandoned many of their Texas missions, and soon thereafter they declared that peace with the Apaches appeared impossible.

Yet attempts at coexistence continued to be made. During 1765–68, the ambitious and innovative Marques de Rubí studied the Apache problem and suggested administrative reforms to solve the dilemma. His efforts resulted in the Royal Regulations of 1772, which did improve frontier conditions slightly. However, in succeeding years skirmishes continued, and the Apaches won most of the battles. By 1786, the harassed Spaniards had finally made progress; from then until 1810, with many Apaches receiving gifts and living in villages established by the Spaniards, conditions improved. There was more stability during these years than there was in any other period in the history of relations between Spaniard and Indian. For the first time there was the possibility of developing villages, and even of opening coal mines, in northwestern Mexico. But in 1810 the Mexican people declared their independence from Spain, and in the war that followed the frontier was rekindled by the flames of Indian warfare.[1]

In September of 1810 a little-known parish priest, Miguel Hidalgo y Castillo, called together his followers and declared Mexico independent of Spain. This early attempt to secure freedom from Spanish domination was followed by other similar proclamations. Yet independence from Spain was not easily acquired, for she had a 300-year-old investment in Mexico and would not readily abdicate her position. Nonetheless, the Mexicans won their independence in 1821, and some stability temporarily returned. But while the deadly struggle for self-determination engulfed the nation in war, the Apaches freely raided in northern and central Mexico. The generally chaotic political climate and the shortage of funds and manpower made immediate reprisals against the Indians impossible. The instability in Mexico doubtless encouraged the Apaches at this time, and it would be an important factor during the second quarter of the nineteenth century, when the division and diffusion of responsibilities among the United States agencies that administered Indian policy opened the frontier to Apache attack.

By 1831 raids had become so incessant in Chihuahua and Sonora, Mexican frontier regions, and attacks on missionary outposts in present-day Arizona and New Mexico so effective, that the Apaches practically came and went without fear of reprisal. Finally, in desperation, the Mexicans evacuated more than 100 towns. Arispe, the major city in Sonora, was threatened with annihilation. These northern Mexicans had suffered deeply, and by 1831 they wanted their government to take decisive action. Moreover, by then the government had achieved sufficient political stability to be able to send soldiers to punish the hostiles. But the Apaches, testing the new government, became even more daring, and the Mexicans were easily intimidated. After fighting several skirmishes, they decided to negotiate with the Indians, hoping for an agreement that would bring peace, if not total victory. Unfortunately, both the military and the civilian leaders of Mexico were so willing to reach a settlement that the Apache and Comanche warriors interpreted their eagerness as a sign of weakness. Thus the effort again proved futile, and frontier Mexicans continued to suffer from Indian attacks, the militia and army remaining ineffective. Wisely, the Apaches rarely fought set battles, but when they did engage in such strategy they calculated the risk and usually succeeded in routing the Mexicans.

Discipline in the frontier forts and all through the region disappeared, for no effective effort could be mounted to tame the renegades. Between 1840 and 1850, Apaches and other nomadic tribes were the unchallenged masters of the region. All the way up to the Mexican–American War of 1846–48, the Apaches bought modern weapons from American traders or took them from victims killed in raids. With the Indians so well mounted and armed, little could be done to defeat them. Suffering, terror, and desolation hung over the Mexican frontier. Neither the Spaniards nor the Mexicans could domesticate these warriors, and when the United States acquired the territory in 1848, the Apaches were still the scourge of the frontier.

General José M. Carasco, the military Governor of Sonora in the 1840's, stated that many of the small settlements to the north had become resigned to defeat and were paying tribute to the raiders, thereby purchasing a respite part of the time. However, Carasco remarked, the Indians who were given supplies in Chihuahua frequently were the same warriors who then went and wreaked havoc on the Sonoran frontier. This patriotic Mexican leader did his best to pursue and strike at the Indians when he learned the location of a stronghold; in one attack in 1850 on Indians visiting Janos, Chihuahua, Carasco claimed that his troops killed at least 130 Indians and captured some ninety more.[2] Carasco also reported that the commanding general in Chihuahua had been so angered at the attack that he later asked the government to reprimand the Sonoran leader. After hearing the evidence, the federal authorities decided that Carasco had acted correctly. Indians thus became the cause of friction between the leaders of the north Mexican states, as they would between Mexico and the United States some years later.

During the 1840's, the province of Chihuahua suffered more bitterly from Apache depredations than did any other area along northern Mexico. Brave hostiles struck within view of towns, killed sheep herders and settlers, and then slipped quietly off to mountain sanctuaries. As a result of the increasing number of raids after 1850, the frontier was all but depopulated. The solution to the Mexican frontier problem, as General Carasco said, was to end the scarcity of population in the border regions. Unfortunately, people could not be induced to move north easily or quickly. The border was too long and the area too vast; even when the Mexican War ended neither the United States nor Mexico could bring about any significant growth in their border population.

As a result of the increasing number of Indian raids during and after the war with the United States, the Mexicans decided that they might well lose yet more territory to the "gringos" if they did not provide a measure of stability. Along the frontier, this stability had been lacking for over 300 years. In the late 1840's the Mexican government finally came to agree with the observation of men such as Carasco—that the answer lay in populating the frontier. Accordingly, in 1848, 1850, and 1852, three Mexican leaders suggested plans to create military or civilian colonies in the northern states. Unfortunately, all three plans either failed to win national approval or never were implemented. In July 1848, Mexican President José Joaquín de Herrera promulgated a colonization law. He proposed to establish military colonies in the northern states along the boundary with the United States. Municipal government was promised, as well as civilian control. The frontier was to be divided into three parts: the Eastern Frontier, to consist of the states of Tamaulipas and Coahuila; the Middle Frontier, the state of Chihuahua; and the Western Frontier, Sonora and Baja California. To keep the Indians near these settlements peaceful, the law called for paying the tribes 10,000 pesos each year. Various incentives were offered to induce Mexicans to move north, including land grants to retired soldiers and special privileges for married colonists. This Mexican law clearly reflected its creators' fear of an American invasion, for it excluded foreigners, except in special cases, from participating.

Founding these colonies proved difficult, and many Mexicans predicted early abandonment of them. Shortages in financing, poor planning, and incessant delays were commonplace, and by 1850 only nine of the eighteen colonies scheduled for the frontier had been established. On the Western Frontier only two of the proposed six colonies had begun operation.

The failure of this attempt prompted Mariano Paredes, in 1850, to suggest yet another colonization plan. A member of the Sonoran legislature, Paredes believed that civilian colonies had to be securely established before organized campaigns from military enclaves against the renegades could be effective. Paredes therefore journeyed to Mexico City to present to Congress a formal plan very similar to that proposed by Herrera—and with better financing.

On August 16, 1850, he spoke to the Mexican Chamber of Deputies and explained his ideas. He suggested an extensive colonization by civilians, and he advocated a comprehensive mercantile development for the entire frontier. Adamantly, he warned the members of the Chamber that they should beware of that "avaricious neighbor" to the north. Although Paredes did suggest elaborate plans for establishing and financing the colonies, the Mexican Chamber appears to have never debated the plan. It definitely was not approved. Certain of the deputies did agree with Paredes about the need for a colonization plan, and considerable informal talk did occur in governmental circles, but no new suggestions were offered for two years.

In January 1852, a third major colonization plan was proposed. Introduced by Juan N. Almonte, a respected soldier and diplomat, this plan had considerable merit. Unlike his predecessors, who had proposed colonization schemes partly to discourage American expansion, Almonte had as his first concern the Indian menace. He believed it necessary to stop aboriginal raids before turning to other problems of settlement. He believed that once this menace was ended, then the interior wastelands, as well as the frontier, could be colonized. This last feature made his plan the most progressive of the era.

Almonte realized the seriousness of frontier conditions. He told his colleagues in government that life in the north was so deplorable that he was surprised anyone lived there. Almonte was not afraid of the United States; rather, he cited the northern neighbor as an example to be emulated. Mexico, he said, at least must do what Americans had done in order to settle the frontier. That country had grown in wealth and population because it had surveyed, priced, and opened its public domain early in its history. Moreover, Almonte urged his government to send agents to Europe to recruit frontier settlers. But Almonte's proposals, like the others made during this period, were never enacted into law.[3]

The scantily populated Mexican frontier continued to be neglected by the national government, while at the same time local politicians vied for power in the various regions. The Spanish government had not tried to understand the Indians and their lifestyle, and Mexican authorities added little to the sympathetic worldview needed for a workable solution. Desperately searching for an answer, Mexican authorities in the border region turned to bounty hunters as early as 1837. In that year James Johnson, an unsavory character, entered into a contract with Governor Leonardo Escalante y Arvizu, of Sonora. In one incident, Johnson loaded a cannon with shrapnel and fired it into an unsuspecting band of Mimbres Apaches. When the acrid cannon smoke cleared, Johnson and his men unsheathed their knives, and the grisly work of taking scalps began. Johnson had been promised 100 pesos by the Governor for each scalp taken. Later in 1837, partly as a result of Johnson's success, Chihuahua likewise agreed to pay bounties, offering cash for the scalps of Indian men, women, and children. North Mexican authorities, tired of trying to deal with the Apaches on the frontier, thought that such activity would bring the Indians to terms, or, at the very least, discourage their raids against innocent civilians. The scalp bounty system solved nothing; rather, it intensified the struggle, encouraging the Indians to retaliate in an equally brutal mutilation of their victims. A generation later Victorio would have his scalp valued at $2000 by the state of Chihuahua.

Scalp hunting became a big business shortly before the Mexican War. Another enterprising entrepreneur was a Scots-Irish soldier of fortune, James Kirker. He entered the business in 1838, organizing a band of twenty-three men to hunt Apache scalps. Kirker led the hunters, well-armed and thirsting for Apache blood, to an Indian village on the upper Gila River, where, in a surprise attack, they collected fifty-five scalps and captured forty-four head of livestock. Kirker's fame spread so rapidly that Governor General José Joaquín Calvo of Chihuahua invited him to the capital city, there to offer him a lucrative contract to hunt Apache scalps. The following year Kirker negotiated a similar contract with the new civilian Governor of the state. Recruiting 200 men, fifty of whom were Mexicans, Kirker promised to teach the Comanches and Apaches a lesson. He asked for, and received, $5000 with which to organize his force; eventually he would be paid $100,000 for his grisly trophies of victory.

Kirker's subsequent attack was equally remunerative. In September 1839 he led his motley crew in a spectacular assault on a group of unsuspecting Apaches at San Fernando de Taos. There he took forty scalps. During the next few months Kirker's fame spread, and the Governor of Durango also offered him bounties for the heads or scalps of hostile Indians. Military officials, jealous of the success of civilian governors, opposed Kirker, and when Francisco García Conde assumed control of Chihuahua in 1840, he was induced by the military to cancel Kirker's contract. Conde changed his mind later in the year, however, for Indian raids became more serious, and he too was forced to employ Kirker and his unsavory methods. Just as later scalp hunters became greedy, so also did Kirker; he realized that the scalps of Mexicans oftentimes looked like Apache scalps, and he began killing *peones* and selling their scalps to the government. To end this chicanery, Conde changed the bounty system; he offered to hire the men to hunt scalps on a dollar-per-day scale. Kirker did not like this restricted payment schedule, and he retired to western Chihuahua, where he watched the Indians defy Mexican authority—and, possibly, encouraged them. It was thought that he even helped the Indians trade their plunder for ammunition and supplies with which to raid the Mexican frontier.

During the next several years the Mexicans again tried to make treaties with the Indians, but then one state would give bribes or goods to the Apaches and Comanches to get them to stop raiding, and that would encourage the Indians in their attacks on the neighboring state. By 1845 conditions had deteriorated so seriously that the Mexican officials decided the only way to control the depredations was to reinstate the scalp bounty system. Governor Angel Trías, however, felt that Kirker had played some part in encouraging these raids, and he issued a directive stating that he would pay $9000 for Kirker's scalp. However, the devious scalp hunter had not survived by being careless. Arranging a truce allowing him to travel to Chihuahua City to see the Governor, Kirker made an agreement whereby he would once again collect Indian scalps.

Kirker quickly figured that $50 per scalp was more valuable than his friendship with Apaches; therefore he gathered a force of 150 men, returned to the Apache village in which he had been living, killed 182 Indians, and appeared in Chihuahua City with his grotesque trophies— including the scalp of his guide, who had been killed in the fight. Kirker not only collected his money, he also received a hero's welcome. He then continued to hunt scalps until shortly after Mexico went to war against the United States. Just twenty-three days after the war began, his last big day of scalp hunting occurred. On July 7, 1846, he attacked Indians near Galeana, Chihuahua, and gathered 148 scalps. Displayed in Chihuahua City, these scalps were later seen by American soldiers entering the city. However, Kirker again incurred the anger of Mexican authorities shortly after this victory, and the government offered a $10,000 reward for his scalp; he decided it best to leave the area. Thereafter, with Kirker no longer a threat, the Indian marauders renewed their attacks on the entire frontier region. They all but depopulated Chihuahua. In 1847, in a futile attempt to control the Indians, the state of Durango, trying to end the raiding of Comanches, offered $200 per scalp, but there was no one to pick up where Kirker had left off, and the program was ineffective.

The Mexican states would not find anything as damaging to the hostiles as the system of paying scalp bounties, and therefore, after the signing of the Treaty of Guadalupe Hidalgo, ending the war with the

United States, the Mexican authorities again turned to bounties. Chihuahua's Ley Quinto (Fifth Law), promulgated on May 25, 1849, and lasting until 1886, provided for scalp bounties. Under this law, live warriors captured and delivered to the capital would bring $250 each. But because of difficulties in getting the hostiles to Chihuahua City, and the fact that a scalp brought only $50 less than did a live Indian, Mexican officials rarely had to pay the higher price. Lesser prices were paid for the scalps of women and children, but the officials seldom quibbled about paying for scalps considered "too young." [4]

Nor was there any difficulty in recruiting scalp hunters; ex-Texas Rangers, disappointed Forty-niners, runaway slaves, even Indians found it easy work and were willing to sharpen their knives. Although some Mexicans were engaged in the "legal" killings, most of the big money-makers were Americans. Kirker was not alone in his success. John Joel Glanton, another of the American opportunists, operated in present-day Arizona and all along the border. Glanton, who was wanted in Texas as an outlaw, found the climate south of the border more to his liking. Periodically hunting for scalps along the Mexican frontier, he also carried on his bloody enterprise north of the international line. For example, he organized some renegades to operate a ferry on the Colorado River—a very handy business for a scalp hunter. Like many in the business before him, he quickly discovered that the Mexicans could not tell one Indian scalp from another—for that matter, they could not tell a Mexican scalp from that of an Apache. Therefore Glanton also began murdering innocent Mexican peasants and selling their scalps. A merciless killer, Glanton always blamed Indians, particularly the Yuma tribe, for any trouble that occurred in the area; although the Yumas were far from peaceful, they were blamed for many murders in which they had taken no part. In 1850 they decided to take revenge for the death of many of their tribesmen; they attacked Glanton's ferry party, killing Glanton and ten of his men. Survivors of this motley gang reached Los Angeles, where they told a pitiful tale of an Indian "massacre." Making the usual response to troubles on the United States frontier, the California government sent troops to punish the Yumas without actually determining what had happened or who had been at fault.

The practice of scalp hunting continued to flourish on both sides of the border. Indians also occasionally participated. And some chiefs even joined in the competitive spirit by offering rewards for the hair of any American or Mexican. At times the scalp hunters turned on each other, seeking to profit by selling the scalps of members of their own gangs who were wounded in battle or who demonstrated less than adequate enthusiasm for the sport. Considerable money was to be made in the business. By the end of 1849, Chihuahua alone had paid $17,896 for scalps; this was not spent over a long period of time, nor does it show what other states had paid for the services of bounty hunters.

As these scalping parties hunted and killed more and yet more Indians, fewer natives were to be found. Moreover, the indiscriminate killing of women and children helped to deplete the scalp supply. As profits began to decline, Kirker, Glanton, and many others intensified the killing of peaceful agricultural Indians and even innocent Mexican *peones*. Finally, Governor Angel Trías of Chihuahua took action. Pressured by those who were tired of Kirker's activities, Trías investigated the frontier regions and found that Indian raids increased when Kirker, Glanton, and their crews were in a specific area. Realizing that the bounty hunters were at the bottom of much of his state's difficulties, Trías offered $8000 for Glanton's head, just as other frontier states in Mexico already had done.[5]

Scalp hunting, a practice designed to curtail the Indian raids, would in fact cause more damage in the long run than any other single remedy the Mexicans attempted. This, combined with lawlessness in New Mexico, dishonesty in government within the Indian Bureau, and other major problems explains why Victorio and his band of Ojo Caliente Apaches refused to remain on a reservation after 1879. They were determined to remain free rather than live under white domination. Likewise, the Indians seemed brutal and sadistic in their raids— but they had practiced their style of warfare for centuries. Now the Apaches, angered at the wrongdoings of Mexicans and Americans, and frustrated at their own plight, set upon brutal retaliation. These hostiles were penetrating as far south as Mazatlán, Sonora, by 1851; during that year the Indians killed more than 200 citizens along the border and caused immeasurable damage to property.

Mexican authorities in northern Mexico, and their counterparts north of the border, were ineffective against marauding hostiles. Scalp hunting and colonization had failed to solve their Indian problem, while disease—including cholera—drought, and numerous bandits disguised as Indians created additional problems for the authorities. Moreover, gold fever prompted hundreds of settlers to leave the Mexican frontier for the gold fields in California, further reducing the frontier population left to fight.

The political chaos that marked Mexico from the end of the war with the United States until the late 1870's also impeded solution of the problem. In 1848 José Joaquín de Herrera had come to office as President, and he was succeeded peacefully in 1851 by José Mariano Arista. These years saw successive peaceful colonization plans advanced as a solution to frontier difficulties. But on January 5, 1853, conservatives overthrew the government. Shortly thereafter, they invited the wily Antonio López de Santa Anna to take over, and within a few months he overthrew the constitution and declared a dictatorship. The frontier provinces were forced to accept this new turn of events; gradually, even General Trías lent his support, and he helped depose Governor José Cordero of Chihuahua. By 1855, Santa Anna's star had declined; Mexican leaders in Chihuahua then promptly declared themselves in favor of the Plan de Ayutla, supported a new federalist constitution, and chose sides in the ensuing War of the Reform.*

During the next few years, while the liberal-conservative conflict engulfed the country, Indians raided and kept the frontier in a state of anarchy. The struggle between liberals and conservatives crippled all

---

* The War of the Reform (1858–61) was a continuation of the Centralist–Federalist struggle. Liberals supported a federal system of government, with circumscription of church and military power, while conservatives fought for the ideal of church and army control.

efforts to contain the Indians. Liberals gained the upper hand in Chihuahua by 1860, and once in control they began to circumscribe the prerogatives of the clergy and make liberal reforms. General Luis Terrazas, a liberal, was chosen as temporary Governor of this northern Mexican province. However, in 1862 French intervention * on the side of the conservatives brought about new political strife. Just as it seemed that stability had returned and a concerted war might be commenced against the hostiles, civil war broke out again and the frontier was reduced to chaos. In 1864, French control was extended to the frontier areas, martial law was decreed in Chihuahua, and Terrazas was removed from power. Finally, as a result of the insistence of the people in the state, Angel Trías, described as a friendly and frank man, again was named Governor. Yet Trías was accused of drinking heavily by the conservatives, and a barrage of criticism prevented his taking effective action. The French gained control of the central provinces and were preparing a final assault on the frontier. The liberal government of Benito Juárez, valiantly fighting against the French, was driven from its temporary quarters at Saltillo and was forced to establish its command center in Chihuahua. Within the next few months the French supporters captured Chihuahua and moved north toward the United States. Juárez fled toward Paso del Norte, as did the liberals.

Fearing contact with troops from the United States, Marshal Francisco A. Bazaine, the French commander in Mexico, ordered his supporters to halt their advance northward. Unable to retain their hold on the region without reinforcements, the pro-French troops withdrew from Chihuahua on October 29, 1865, leaving the area to a reinstated Governor, the popular Luis Terrazas. In December of that year, at Emperor Maximilian's order, the province of Chihuahua was reoccupied, but again it could not be held. By mid-1866, Mexican liberals

---

* The French had been interested in Mexico for several years. While the United States fought a Civil War, France placed Maximilian, an Austrian nobleman, on the "throne" of Mexico as Emperor. Controlling sections of Mexico directly or indirectly between 1862 and 1867, the French intended to remain masters of Mexico. With the end of the Civil War, the United States pressured for French withdrawal. The last French troops left Mexico in September 1867.

were in control of the state again, and again they declared it free. In a general election held in 1867, Luis Terrazas was confirmed as Governor of the province, and he seemed capable of keeping the peace. Unfortunately, the temporary stability in Chihuahua did not reflect the over-all situation in Mexico.

Benito Juárez, who had been confirmed as President of Mexico in the elections of 1867, was bitterly opposed by the conservatives. From 1867 to 1871 a renewed civil war shaped the Mexican political scene. While in the midst of this war the Mexicans were unwilling to fight or deal fairly with the Indians of the border states. In the election of 1871 Juárez was re-elected, but a military candidate, the popular Porfirio Díaz, claimed the election was fraudulent, and he began a revolution to overthrow the government, thereby invalidating the results. Díaz' supporters maintained control of Chihuahua for a short time, but in the middle of 1872 Juárez died, and Díaz relinquished his control. Peace and stability were restored for a short time. Governor Terrazas, who had been the leader in the state, resigned, and Antonio Ochoa became the provincial leader. All appeared relatively calm until the election of 1875.

In major elections that year the followers of Porfirio Díaz, known as the Porfiristas, renewed hostilities and the frontier again was engulfed in war. Again no effort was made to control the Indians. In June of 1876 the aging Chihuahuan leader Angel Trías spearheaded a movement to overthrow the government. However, the Porfiristas succeeded all along the frontier, capturing states and holding them for Díaz. A rival faction, known as the Lerdist party, was driven from Mexico into the United States; its adherents invaded the northern Mexican states again in 1877, and they occupied Paso del Norte (Ciudad Juárez) for a short time before they were driven back across the border. A crop failure, which was made worse by a drought that lasted several years, caused considerable suffering and ill feelings toward the ruling elites in the northern areas. Revolution again flamed when Trías, then in control in Chihuahua, was accused of misappropriating funds and violating the state constitution. Full-scale revolution returned to the northern frontier.[6]

Jesus José Casavantes headed the revolutionary forces in Chihuahua, and in August of 1879 he proclaimed the removal of Trías. Casavantes briefly occupied the capital, but federal troops arrived and arrested him. Still, Casavantes had a measure of success, for when the federal government deposed him, Trías was removed from office. In November, Luis Terrazas was called to become Governor again. Terrazas, who controlled Chihuahua until 1884, desperately wanted to solve the Indian problem. He began the campaign to defeat the Apache war chief Victorio. Thereafter, the Porfiristas were nominally in control in the states along the international border, but quarrels between the individual provinces over water, raids by isolated bands of opponents seeking to create havoc, and fights over mining rights kept the frontier in turmoil. Not until 1880 did the border provinces adequately prepare for a campaign against the hostile Indians, who were then raiding both sides of the international border. After assuming the governorship in 1879, Terrazas wasted no time getting to the matter of subjugating Victorio's band. The new Governor was a liberal, but so too was Díaz—according to the Porfiristas. Sporadic revolutionary outbreaks occurred afterwards, but political stability did improve the frontier situation. Military forces could be concentrated in isolated areas to help end Indian and frontier difficulties.

The Apaches continued to be an issue in both Mexico and the United States. From their first contact with the indigenous population of the Southwest, whites had failed to find an equitable solution to a tragic dilemma. From the time of the Spanish entrance to the Mexican Cession agreement, neither original ideas nor sincere efforts to understand the culture and deeds of the Indian were advanced by the conquerors of the region. The only attitude displayed was that of hostile whites against equally hostile Indians, both sides unwilling or unable to resolve their differences peacefully. Mexican authorities were so involved in internal conflicts that governments lasted only hours or days, and the continued inability to contain the Indians was but an expression of the life-and-death political struggle engulfing Mexico. Moreover, when Mexicans attempted to solve the problem, they almost always used retaliatory actions, or temporary solutions at best. Most harmful to relations between the groups was the practice of offering bounties for scalps, for this brutal policy prompted Indians to retaliate in an equally brutal fashion.[7]

Peace was impossible in a region with an artificial international boundary, Americans on one side claiming ownership, Mexicans on the other claiming ownership, and Apaches in between living on the land as they had done before Columbus sailed from Spain. Chaos, political instability, war, struggles for power, greed, graft, and corruption: these were the "civilized" practices of representatives of the three peoples that in turn contested for the Apache homeland.

2
A CLASH OF CULTURES

As the year 1846 approached, southern New Mexico and Arizona were still largely the domain of the Apache, who roamed there at will and without fear. Little did he care about ownership of the land in the European legal sense; he knew the land was his, and he took what he wanted. For centuries he had raided the other tribes of the region, just as he had the Spaniards when they settled in northern Mexico and the Rio Grande Valley. In the early years of the nineteenth century the Apache met few Americans—fur trappers, explorers, and those hardy souls heading westward toward California—but they posed no threat to him or his way of life. He continued to ride his war trails with his fellow Apaches, following whatever leader inspired him. Swooping down on Mexican villages or the encampments of other Indians, he drove off livestock, stole food, and enslaved women and children. Life was good, the gods were kind, and the land seemed beautiful.

Then came the Treaty of Guadalupe Hidalgo, and the traditional homeland of the Apaches became United States territory. An artificial boundary line between Mexico and the United States was created, drawn up by men who neither understood nor ever considered the predatory nature of the Apaches, nor grasped their inability to understand the white man's concept of national boundaries. Moreover, Article XI of the agreement obligated the United States to halt raids into Mexico by Indians living north of the new boundary, making conflict between the Indians and the Americans inevitable. This provision proved to be not only unrealistic, as Americans quickly learned, but unenforceable. There was no way the Army could halt the Apache raids; the Indians were constantly moving, and the country was remote, an unexplored and unmapped desert, too vast for the few soldiers assigned to the area to patrol effectively.

While the Indians saw the boundary as an artificial dividing line, one based on political considerations rather than social or geographical reality, Americans and Mexicans treated it as a symbol of national honor, thereby compounding the difficulty of ending the raiding. Mexican officials—and civilians just to the south of the boundary—would not cooperate with the Americans, while the Mexican Army was incapable of giving any help. The Mexican government stoutly refused to allow American soldiers to cross this boundary, even when in hot pursuit of raiding hostiles. And American officials certainly did not want columns of mounted and armed Mexicans setting foot on American soil. Each nation preferred to believe that it could solve the problem without the help of the other.

Into this morass of traditional Indian behavior, treaty obligations, and national chauvinism came James S. Calhoun, who received his commission as Superintendent of Indian Affairs for New Mexico in April 1849. Born in 1802, Calhoun had fought in the recent war with Mexico as a lieutenant colonel of Georgia volunteers; he was a staunch Whig and an admirer of Zachary Taylor. When Taylor became President, he rewarded Calhoun with the $1500-a-year position in New Mexico. Calhoun came down the Santa Fe Trail in company with a detachment of soldiers, arriving at the New Mexican capital city on July 22. His orders were to gather statistical data and other information that would make possible better relations with the Indians living in the territory.

At first Calhoun felt he could improve U.S. relations with the Apaches through better communications (as he likewise hoped to do with the Navajos). Within three months, he would gather information that would turn his naïveté to dismay. In his assessment of conditions in New Mexico that summer of 1849, he reported to his superiors in Washington that it was impossible to travel ten miles outside any New Mexican village without fear of an Indian attack. Within a short time he would argue, as would his successors, that the only way to contain the Apaches was to harass them to the point of surrender and then to place them on reservations. The Apaches should be made totally dependent on the government; this would make them sedentary and, eventually, would force them to adopt the ways of the white man. Calhoun, on March 3, 1851, became the first Governor of the newly created Territory of New Mexico. He also continued in his position as Superintendent of Indian Affairs. By 1852, three years after coming to the Territory, he was forced to write Secretary of State Daniel Webster that the Apaches were openly attacking American troops and that no one, not even the soldier in his barracks, was immune.[1]

Calhoun's attempts to make peace with the Indians were repeated in the next decade, but the Apaches continued to be the real masters of the land. In the southern part of New Mexico and in southern Arizona, the two tribes of Apaches that were the most belligerent were the Chiricahua and the Mescalero. Mangas Coloradas, leader of the Apaches who controlled southwestern New Mexico, was considered by many people in that territory to have been the greatest Apache war chief of the nineteenth century. He was born sometime between 1790 and 1795 in southern New Mexico. At manhood he stood six feet, two inches, an impressive figure who rose to prominence and then leadership. His raids against Apache enemies were so well planned and executed that he became a legend of fear in his own lifetime. For thirty years, until his death in 1863, he was the scourge of northern Mexico and the southwestern United States.[2]

One insight into Mangas Coloradas' attitude came in 1852, when he, along with some other Apache chieftains, was negotiating a treaty with the United States. Major John Greiner, one of the Americans there, asked him why the Apaches attacked the Mexicans so violently and so repeatedly. The Apache chief replied eloquently on the subject of Mexican treachery, saying that some of his people had once been invited to a fiesta at a Mexican village; there they were given too much to drink and then were systematically clubbed to death. He added that at other times Mexicans had concealed cannon and other weapons and had fired into unsuspecting groups of Indians. Because of such treachery he could never live in peace with Mexicans.[3]

Mangas Coloradas had sufficient vision to realize the advantages of unity among the various sub-tribes of Apaches, and through the marriage of his three daughters he sought to cement relations between his own Mimbres tribe and neighboring bands. The only one of these alliances that proved effective was that made with Cochise, a leader of the Chiricahua. Cochise was born about 1823, in southern New Mexico. In 1870 he was described as standing "five feet nine and one-half inches high; . . . weight 164 pounds; broad shoulders; stout frame; eyes medium size and very black; hair straight and black . . . ; scarred all over the body with buckshot; very high forehead; large nose, and for an Indian straight." Like Mangas Coloradas, Cochise was a bitter enemy of Mexicans and fought them constantly. However, he was friendly toward the first Americans to come into the Southwest and would continue to be so until just before the Civil War.[4]

Late in 1860, a band of marauding Apaches struck an isolated ranch in the Sonoita Valley of southern Arizona. The owner, John Ward, lived there with his Mexican mistress and her children by previous "husbands." One of these youngsters, Felix (who later would gain fame under the name Mickey Free), disappeared during the attack. It is not known whether he ran away or was captured by the Indians. Ward went to near-by Fort Buchanan to complain to the authorities that Cochise and the Chiricahuas had stolen the lad, as well as some cattle. Late in January 1861, Lieutenant George N. Bascom and fifty-four soldiers were sent to demand the lad's return. They marched to Apache Pass, and when Cochise and several of his men came into their camp Bascom demanded that the boy be freed. Cochise insisted that he knew nothing of the raid, whereupon Bascom said he would

Cochise, the Chiricahua Apache chief. From a painting, artist unknown. *Western History Collections, University of Oklahoma Library.*

General E. R. S. Canby, Union Commander in New Mexico during the Civil War. *Western History Collections, University of Oklahoma Library.*

hold the Indian chief hostage until the youngster was returned. Cochise thereupon cut his way out of the tent and, dodging bullets, escaped alone into the hills. Soon warriors surrounded Bascom's camp, and the lieutenant sent for more troops. Later there was an attempted exchange of prisoners, but this failed, several whites were murdered, and three of Cochise's close relatives were hanged. This "Bascom Affair" caused warfare to begin in earnest between Cochise's Chiricahua Apaches and the Americans.[5]

To contend with these Indians—and the white traders who exchanged whiskey and other goods for the livestock stolen by the Apaches in their raids—the Army had only two military posts in Arizona prior to the Civil War: Fort Buchanan, on the Sonoita River, and Fort Breckenridge, on the San Pedro River. Both were understaffed, and the troops poorly equipped. Fort Buchanan was not stockaded, and at night Apaches could roam freely around the adobe buildings. Then came the Civil War, and the Union forces were withdrawn from even these two posts. Cochise and Mangas Coloradas became almost total masters of southwestern New Mexico and southeastern Arizona, raiding without hindrance and stealing from Mexicans and Americans alike. In the summer of 1861 Colonel E. R. S. Canby, the Union commander in New Mexico, reported that Indian attacks were becoming more severe every day and that peace would not come until all hostiles were forced onto reservations. However, he could not accomplish this because of a Confederate invasion.[6]

Colonel John Robert Baylor, who was named Governor of the Confederate Territory of Arizona, disagreed somewhat with Canby's assessment. Arriving in July of 1861 at Mesilla, Baylor concluded that the only solution was a campaign of total extermination, a concept in keeping with his background. Born in Kentucky in 1822, he completed grammar school and even briefly attended a university in Cincinnati before moving to Texas in 1840. There he became a member of the famed Texas Rangers and enthusiastically fought the Comanches, a pastime he subsequently continued as a rancher near Weatherford (thirty miles west of Fort Worth). At the outbreak of the Civil War he was elected lieutenant colonel of the Texas Mounted Volunteers, and he led troops to capture El Paso. From El Paso he launched an attack on southern New Mexico, and there he assumed the governorship of what he called the Territory of Arizona (all of present New Mexico and Arizona south of the 34th parallel). Late in 1861, Baylor was super-

seded as military commander in the region by Brigadier General Henry H. Sibley, who came to conquer and govern New Mexico. Sibley, a graduate of West Point and a former Army officer, was more concerned with fighting Union troops than Indians, but he favored enslaving Indians rather than exterminating them.

Despite the philosophical differences between the two Confederate commanders, Baylor sent orders to the troops operating between Mesilla and Tucson to "use all means to persuade the Apaches or any tribe to come in for the purpose of making peace, and when you get them together kill all the grown Indians and take the children prisoners and sell them to defray the expense of killing the Indians." [7] Such an approach hardly was designed to bring peace, and it did not. Before the Confederates could achieve any final solution—or even an approach to one—they were driven out by the California Column, a detachment of volunteers fighting under the Union flag.

Commanding the California Column was Brigadier General James H. Carleton. He drove both Baylor and Sibley from Arizona and New Mexico, ridding both areas of all Confederates. Once that was accomplished, he too had to face the Apache problem. Carleton found himself in sympathy with Baylor's approach: the only way to control the Indians, he decided, was to kill all the men and to imprison the women and children. Fortunately, he did not have sufficient men to accomplish his ends. He did pause on his first march through the Southwest to erect Fort Bowie, to pressure the Chiricahuas into making peace. Once in New Mexico, he conceived more ambitious plans against the Mimbres and other Apaches.

He sent soldiers on a sweep of the country around the Santa Rita copper mines, and there, early in 1863, Mangas Coloradas was captured. According to the official report of what followed, the aged Indian chief was killed shortly after his capture, when he tried to rush a guard. Other reports, given by private soldiers, sound more plausible.

General John R. Baylor, Confederate Commander of the Territory of Arizona during the Civil War, 1870's. *Western History Collections, University of Oklahoma Library.*

According to them, Mangas Coloradas was lured into the army camp on the pretext of making peace, but instead was arrested. That night Brigadier General J. R. West, who was in command of the troops, told his men that the chief was a murderer who had "got away from every soldier command and has left a trial of blood for five hundred miles on the old [Butterfield] stage line. I want him dead or alive tomorrow morning, do you understand. *I want him dead.*" [8] The next morning Mangas Coloradas was found shot—an event that stirred his followers to even greater hatred and distrust of Americans.

In March 1863 Carleton's troops captured so many Apaches that the general ordered the construction of a reservation at Bosque Redondo, a site on the Pecos River in east-central New Mexico. More than 400 Mescalero Apaches were quartered there. In the fall and winter of 1863–64, Carleton sent men to crush the Navajos, and when this was accomplished they also were taken to Bosque Redondo. Yet Carleton, for all his pretensions to greatness and his aspirations for high political office, was unable to conquer all the Apaches or stop their raiding. He could not place the Territory under an umbrella of troops; to achieve peace would have taken either a great negotiator and peacemaker or a far larger army than was at his disposal. Both Arizona, which became a separate Territory by an act of Congress in 1863, and New Mexico remained fearful of Apache war cries.

The end of the Civil War found New Mexico and Arizona remote and little understood or appreciated by the mass of Americans. Few whites called this desert-mountain country home, for only a scant handful of pioneers saw the beauty and the economic potential of the area. When these few cried for protection of their lives and homes from Apache terror, Congressmen and the President saw little reason to listen, for residents of the territories could not vote in either congressional or presidential elections. Thus the complaints of the delegates to Congress from these two territories were forwarded to the Army, which was told to find a solution satisfactory to all concerned.

From the start, the effort on the part of the Army to end the wars of the Southwest was hampered by lack of coordination. In 1865, Arizona became a district under the Department of California, while New Mexico remained a separate military department. Thus one commander might be fighting in New Mexico while another was negotiating in Arizona—or the reverse. Moreover, in Arizona, beginning in 1865, civilian volunteers were recruited to fight under twelve-month contracts; from the white point of view these men were gallant and effective, for they proved ruthless in pursuing Apache raiders. But when the Indians became too hard pressed, they would go to the nearest agent of the Bureau of Indian Affairs to ask for peace and protection, which were granted. No real solution was possible in the Southwest, given the division of authority between the two departments and the two agencies of government that were responsible for the Indians.

Also complicating the picture was the peace policy instituted by Ulysses S. Grant when he became President in March of 1869. Grant believed that all Indians should be placed on reservations that would be administered by agents named by the various religious denominations (his concept was labeled the "Quaker Policy"). Many of these agents refused to accept information that contradicted their initial determination even when firsthand evidence was available; they naïvely believed that brotherly love was the only requirement for a solution to the Indian problem in the Southwest. To oversee the implementation of this policy, Grant named General Ely Parker Commissioner of Indian Affairs. The President confidently expected Parker to place all Indians on reservations with a minimum of difficulty.[9]

Parker came to his office with great enthusiasm and optimism. He fired most of the agents previously appointed, sending west agents who had been recommended by the various religious denominations. Learning that there was corruption in virtually every government office that had dealings with the Indians, he created a Board of Indian Commissioners, composed of private citizens, to serve as a guiding board and to examine the activities of the Bureau of Indian Affairs. He also secured from the President an order forbidding soldiers to set foot on any reservation without the express invitation of the resident Indian agent. Yet this only complicated the problem, for it again divided the authority. On the reservation the agent was supreme; he could—and many did—cheat the Indians and degrade their heritage until many fled what they saw as a prison. Then the soldier was ordered to bring them back; when he succeeded he was called a tyrant, and when he failed he was called incompetent.

On April 15, 1870, Arizona was separated from the Department of California, becoming a department in its own right. Brigadier General George Stoneman was sent to take charge of this new unit. Stoneman tried to enforce the President's decision to place all natives on reservations, where they were to become quasi-members of white civilization. Yet to get the Indians onto reservations required fighting, and within five months Stoneman's troops had killed more than 200 hostiles and had made life unpleasant for hundreds of other natives in the Territory. Nevertheless, his efforts still failed to satisfy the local civilians, who wanted all the Indians exterminated, not placed on reservations. On April 30, 1871, some of the dissatisfied citizens took the matter into their own hands.

In February 1871, some 300 Aravaipa Apaches, led by their chief, Eskiminzin, arrived at Camp Grant, Arizona, where they expressed a strong wish to settle on a reservation. Inasmuch as the local commander—even the departmental commander—had no orders covering such a situation, the request had to be sent to Washington for response. In the interim the Apaches settled peacefully near the camp to wait. Unfortunately, sporadic raids continued, raids committed by Apaches other than those led by Eskiminzin; in fact, hostiles even attacked Tucson, driving off stock and killing settlers.

The local citizens insisted the the raiders were from the supposedly peaceful Arivaipa Apaches—and possibly a few young warriors from the tribe did follow some war chief on forays and then return to the safety of Eskiminzin's camp. The angry Tucsonians got together and appointed commissioners to meet with General Stonemen, commander of the Department of Arizona, and demand the removal of the Arivaipas; Stoneman replied that he could not help them and suggested that they band together to protect themselves. Under the leadership of

William S. Oury and Jesus M. Elías, two respected residents of the town, 148 men secretly met. Forty-eight of them were Mexicans, ninety-four were Papago Indians, and six were Anglo-Americans. Armed with clubs, knives, and guns, they slipped out of Tucson in small numbers to avoid detection. They rendezvoused east of town on April 28, and, two days later, as the first streaks of dawn brightened the desert sky, they attacked the unsuspecting Aravaipa Apaches. More than 100 Apaches were killed in this vicious attack, only eight of them men; twenty-nine children were brought to Tucson as prisoners or else sold by the Papagos into slavery in Sonora. The "Red Devils," according to the citizens of Tucson, had been punished for their dastardly deeds. The local residents saw nothing wrong with killing children of the Indians; an Indian child who lived would soon be a warrior.[10]

Easterners who sympathized with the Indians were indignant at what was labeled the "Camp Grant Massacre." President Grant was so angered that he ordered the arrest and trial of those involved in the incident. They were arrested; however, no jury of Arizonans would convict anyone for killing an Indian, and all were freed in short order. Beyond this, the Camp Grant Massacre made federal officials realize that a solution had to be found. The southwestern tribes could not be ignored, nor could they be dealt with on an individual basis, as they had been prior to the Civil War. Grant therefore responded by sending a peace commission to Arizona with instructions to arrange treaties with the Apaches that would place all of them on reservations.

Heading this commission was Vincent Colyer, a Quaker. From the start, his work was hampered by the hostility of Arizona civilians. Even Governor A. P. K. Safford, a Vermonter by birth, expressed opposition to the reservation concept and stated that the peace commissioner entertained "erroneous" opinions of Indians; Stafford preferred the raising and arming of volunteer companies of civilians who would hunt the Indians to exhaustion—if not extermination. Despite the opposition, however, Colyer proceeded quietly with his task. Within a year he had placed nearly 4000 Indians on reservations; it was he who established San Carlos as the principal preserve for Apaches. When his work was done, the only major tribe still free was the Chiricahua Apache. The responsibility for these Indians fell within the province of the army and its commander in the territory, Lieutenant Colonel George Crook.

Born in Ohio on September 8, 1828, Crook, after completing his high school education, went on to West Point. Four years later, in 1852, he was graduated. He served for nine years in California prior to the outbreak of the Civil War. The war gave him the opportunity to display his abilities, and he advanced rapidly in rank. He became colonel of the thirty-eighth Ohio Volunteers and was later breveted a major general of volunteers. At the end of the war he reverted to his permanent rank of lieutenant colonel. He was sent to Idaho Territory, where he served until June 4, 1871, when he was assigned to command the Department of Arizona.[11]

A study of Apache warfare convinced Crook that the Army would have to make dramatic changes in its methods if it hoped to compete with the hostiles. The best way to pursue the Apaches, he decided, was to copy their techniques of rapid movement; therefore he used mules rather than wagons to carry supplies, cut the amount of provisions carried, and trained his troops in the mechanics of long and rapid campaigns. Moreover, Crook concluded that the best trackers of Indians were other Indians; he enlisted natives into the Army for six-month terms as scouts. Such scouts were easy to secure, for the various tribes had ancient animosities; when one group began raiding, he would go among their enemies and enlist them. They were eager to settle their own old scores.

When Colyer departed Arizona, Crook was ready to test his theories in the field. However, yet another peace commission arrived, and he had to wait. This one was headed by General Oliver Otis Howard, a veteran of the Civil War and the Indian wars—and a deeply religious man. The troops said of Howard that he had lost one arm in the Civil War and carried a Bible under the remaining one; he was known as "The Christian General" and "Bible-quoting Howard." Whatever his religious convictions, Howard soon convinced the soldiers that he was efficient at his new task. He held conferences with the Pima, the Papago, and several Apache bands and persuaded them to move to the reservations. Then, through the efforts of Thomas J. Jeffords, a white man whom Cochise trusted, Howard arranged a face-to-face confrontation with the leader of the Chiricahua Apaches. By treaty, the Chiricahuas agreed to settle on a reservation; this centered on the Sulphur Springs, Dragoon, and Chiricahua Mountains, the traditional homeland of the tribe. They lived up to the treaty until 1874, the year Cochise died.[12]

Once Howard concluded his negotiations, Crook was free to contend with the remaining hostiles. In a winter campaign in 1872–73 his soldiers relentlessly pursued the non-reservation Indians. The last of them, the Yavapais, finally surrendered at Camp Verde (in northwestern Arizona) in April 1873. Crook's theories of warfare in the desert Southwest had been fully vindicated by his spectacular achievement, for which he was promoted—from lieutenant colonel to brigadier general! A period of relative peace then settled on Arizona; all the Indian tribes were on reservations.

In 1875 Crook was transferred north to participate in the wars against the Sioux. Just as he was leaving the Southwest, a new Indian agent, John P. Clum, was sent to Arizona to take charge of the Apache reservation at San Carlos. Clum, only twenty-three years old, and a member of the Dutch Reformed Church, was born near Claverack, New York, in 1851. He came to New Mexico in 1871 to manage a meteorological station maintained by the Signal Corps at Santa Fe, a position he held until moving to Arizona.

Clum arrived at San Carlos just as the Bureau of Indian Affairs was trying to move all Apaches—4000 of them—to that reservation. One danger in this was their very number—up to that time the land had supported only 800 Apaches. Moreover, these sub-tribes of Apaches who were supposed to live as neighbors were deadly enemies. Clum tried to relieve the pressures that were building by organizing an agency police force consisting of twenty-five Apaches. And he al-

Indian Agent John P. Clum with Indian policemen Diablo and Eskiminzin. San Carlos Agency, 1875. *National Archives.*

lowed Apaches to serve as their own judges and juries. For three years, until his resignation in 1877, Clum maintained an uneasy peace at San Carlos.[13]

During this same period there also was a search for peace in New

Mexico. Raids were commonplace there immediately following the Civil War, and the Army seemed incapable of winning peace on the field of battle. Civilians in that territory, as in Arizona, grew tired of the raids and the excuses of military commanders; however, they did nothing so spectacular as a Camp Grant Massacre. Rather, they contented themselves with writing letters of complaint to their territorial representative in Congress and to the Santa Fe *Weekly New Mexican.* Many of these letter writers suggested that the government might bring peace by renewing the old Spanish system of paying bounties for Indian scalps, as the governments of the Mexican states of Sonora and Chihuahua were then doing.

The military commanders of the Department of New Mexico did attempt to halt the raiders, but largely through the erection of forts at strategic points. Fort Selden was established at the southern end of the *Jornada del Muerte* early in 1865; its purpose was to protect the Mesilla Valley. Fort Bayard was constructed near Silver City to protect the miners. Patrols were constantly in the field trying to discourage Indian attacks. Moreover, militia groups were formed in New Mexico to combat the hostiles, another practice dating from the time when the Spanish flag flew in the province. Forts, patrols, and militia combined to harass the Apaches of southern New Mexico so that they would move onto one of the reservations, principal among which was Bosque Redondo.

On the reservation at Bosque Redondo were confined the Mescaleros, whom General Carleton had captured in 1863, and the Navajos, who had surrendered to him in 1864. These two tribes were bitter enemies, and quarrels between them were frequent. In 1865 the Mescaleros fled to the frontier, where they began raiding anew. Three years of fighting followed, during which time various commanders questioned the wisdom of quartering Navajos and Apaches on the same reservation. Finally, in 1868, General William T. Sherman, commanding general of the Army, visited the area and ordered that the Navajos be permitted to return to their traditional homeland in northwestern New Mexico and northeastern Arizona.[14]

Then, in 1869, President Grant instituted his peace policy. Charles E. Drew was assigned as Indian agent for southern New Mexico, with orders to solve the problems in the region. When he arrived, he learned that the hostiles, principally the Ojo Caliente Apaches, wanted their own reservation, one separate from the other Indians and even from other sub-tribes of Apaches. Chief Loco wanted to live at Cuchillo Negro, a traditional hunting ground for his tribe on the east side of the Mimbres Mountains. Drew saw no reason to oppose this, and he met with Loco and the chiefs of the Ojo Caliente, including Victorio; however, he could not allay their fears that the government at some future date might reverse such a decision and move them elsewhere. Moreover, Drew could not supply them with the commodities they needed if they were to settle into a sedentary life. Finally, he could do nothing to convince the local civilians that these Apaches would be peaceful, just as Loco and Victorio could not halt isolated raids by young warriors from their own and other Apache bands. Drew therefore had little chance of success as he tried to implement the peace policy. Nevertheless, the Ojo Caliente settled near Cañada Alamosa, at a site later set aside (1874) as the Ojo Caliente reservation, and Drew breathed a sign of relief.

Conflicts started almost immediately. W. L. Rynerson, who figured in the Lincoln County War and was post trader at Fort Bayard, publicly accused the Ojo Caliente of raiding and then slipping back to their reservation for safety; the Indian enclave was nothing more than a protected area where the Indians could not be punished, he declared. Civilians in the near-by towns agreed with Rynerson, and they began pressing for a change in the government's policy; they wanted the Indians moved elsewhere—which almost guaranteed the failure of the experiment. Following loud protests from these civilians, the number of raids did lessen in ensuing months.

Unfortunately for the Ojo Caliente Apaches, Drew died on June 5,

Loco, Ojo Caliente Apache chief. *National Archives.*

1870, while in the mountains seeking to confer with renegade Mescaleros. The new agent, A. G. Hennisee, assessed the local situation upon his arrival and decided that no solution was possible. In November 1870, after coming to blows with inefficient and negligent officials at Cañada Alamosa, he was succeeded by Orland F. Piper, who had been sponsored by the Presbyterian Board of Foreign Missions. Piper likewise proved unable to control events.[15]

All along the New Mexican frontier trouble was brewing among the irate civilians. Fearful of the real and imagined consequences of quartering warlike Indians on reservations within their midst, these local citizens threatened to act in the name of peace if the government did not. Just as Tucsonians had attacked the Indians at Camp Grant, New Mexicans threatened to strike at Indians encamped near them. Territorial Governor William A. Pile liked the peace policy, but he was influenced by the public's fear and hatred of the hostiles. He threatened to yield to the citizens' pressure and strike against the Indians if the government did not immediately settle the difficulties. More than 1000 Indians were assembled in Cañada Alamosa, and Superintendent Nathaniel Pope was doing his best to keep them there. He had even incurred $9000 in debts in order to help the Indians, but still no supplies were forthcoming from the government.[16]

Early in March of 1871, the Superintendent visited his wards and learned they were expecting scouting parties of armed whites to visit their camp area. Piper had promised the Indians that they had nothing to fear, and he reported to the citizens of New Mexico that if the Indians were not bothered, and if they were given their allotment of food, they would cause no trouble. While searching for food and supplies, however, some of these Indians raided surrounding settlements, sometimes returning to the reservation, but more often hiding in the near-by mountains. Livestock was stolen and citizens were killed. The local residents organized a posse to retrieve the stolen goods and punish those guilty of the killings. However, the Superintendent found exactly the reservation site he wanted, along the Tularosa River in southwestern New Mexico. Soon thereafter he ordered Agent Piper to collect his charges and move them to this general area. Cochise, Loco, and Victorio, then at Cañada Alamosa, did not know that President Grant already had approved the new reservation site; for the government, the only remaining problem was the difficult task of persuading the Apaches, many of whom had returned to Cañada Alamosa, to settle at Tularosa.

The Indians, when finally approached, refused to comply, and Piper recommended that, because of previous difficulties and the cost of forcing tribes, they should be allowed to remain where they were, at least until the spring of 1872. Eventually, after being reassured that no scouts or Army troops would be sent to interfere with them, many of the Indians agreed to go to the new Tularosa reservation. Only Cochise refused. Fortunately, General Oliver Otis Howard arrived in the Southwest at this time; he settled the issue by granting Cochise and his band their own reservation, in the southeastern corner of Arizona. But Howard misinformed the New Mexican Apaches; he promised that they could eventually return to Cañada Alamosa—a promise that the government would not keep. Discontent was rife at Tularosa, for the Indians still wanted to return to their former hunting grounds.

From time to time various agents imposed strict controls on the Apaches, but even when there were few restrictions, the residents of the new reservation longed for earlier days and former homes. In the spring of 1874, after considerable deliberation, the new Indian superintendent, Colonel L. E. Dudley, recommended that the Tularosa reservation be abandoned and its occupants be moved to Ojo Caliente, at the head of Cañada Alamosa. On April 9, 1874, an executive order effecting the transfer was issued from Washington, and by the late summer of 1874, nearly 400 Indians had been moved to this new location. Superficially, all was well. The Governor of the Territory announced that as far as he knew there had been almost no killings or raids after the tribes were allowed to live in their original homeland, and that, although fewer attacks did occur, the fact that they occurred at all indicated that some of the Indians obviously were not complying with agreements. While the plans were discussed to quarter Apaches at

Guardhouse, Fort San Carlos, Ariz., with Apache scouts, *c.* 1880's. *Western History Collections, University of Oklahoma Library.*

Ojo Caliente, there were suggestions that all Indians be placed in Arizona, on the San Carlos Reservation.

Local disagreements over just what to do in any particular instance were often colored by the already established prejudices of the citizens of New Mexico. Their attitude toward Indians, agents, and government policy remained one of constant animosity throughout the last third of the nineteenth century. S. M. Ashenfelter, editor of the *Silver City Herald,* expressed the general view in his condemnation of Indian policy as "criminally absurd." The government should not treat Indian tribes as independent nations, he insisted; "it would be just as sensible to treat with a band of horse-thieves or brigands, who might be preying upon our citizens or with communists, who throng our cities, and only bide their time, to destroy the property of others." The reservation system was likewise condemned. Ashenfelter believed that these preserves were hotbeds "of corruption as far as the agent and his strikers are concerned, and a "temple of refuge" for marauding bands of Indians. . . ." [17] Such bias, although somewhat justifiable, doubtless, added to the problems of the Indians, the agents, and everyone else who along the way had the opportunity to resolve differences.

By the spring of 1876 it was obvious that the peaceful situation in New Mexico would not continue. The financial difficulties of the government, which prevented agents from supplying Indians with meat and grain, and the decision to move Cochise's band to San Carlos all brought about new outbreaks of violence. The great Indian leader had died in 1874, but his people remained together for the next two years at the Chiricahua reservation in southeast Arizona. Before the end of the first quarter of 1876, the government notified agents to lay off employees and to inform all concerned that there would be no quarterly supply of beef and other necessities for the reservation. In April many of the tribes that had once been stationed at Ojo Caliente started moving closer to Cañada Alamosa, in order to fight against their removal to San Carlos. As the Army had a serious stake in this area, Colonel Edward Hatch and Inspector E. C. Kemble of the Indian Bureau jour-

Malpi Station, N.M., one of the lonely stations that hostiles often attacked. *Western History Collections, University of Oklahoma Library.*

neyed to the region to solve the problem. Troops were stationed along the Arizona and New Mexico borders with orders to intercept the Chiricahuas and return them. When Hatch arrived at the reservation he found that many Indians were still there, but they were angry at the continued white duplicity and vacillations of policy, and therefore were heavily armed for the fight.

These Indians, most of whom were peaceful even under intense suffering, had decided that their own methods of finding food were preferable to the government's method, under which they were slowly starving. Kemble then ordered sufficient beef purchased to keep the Apaches calm, but no lasting solution was reached. Hatch suggested, as did other Army officers before and after him, that the only way to control the hostiles was to disarm and dismount them, thereby stopping their wanderings. Only then, he insisted, could these Indians be watched closely and made to begin peaceful farming. This was not done, however, for officials feared that strong tactics would send the tribes into Mexico, from which they could strike at will against settlements on either side of the international border.

The Apaches who lived south of Cañada Alamosa soon came in limited numbers to the Ojo Caliente reservation for beef. There they remained while the government again deliberated their future. During the summer and early fall of 1876, conditions remained unsettled, rations were in short supply, and army scouting parties stayed in the field to keep the Indians at proper locations. Outlaws in the region also created problems for the Indians, for these lawless men raided Indian stock, killed an occasional brave, and were a constant thorn in the sides of both the Army and the Indians. Moreover, territorial conflicts between white settlers, such as the Lincoln County War, complicated matters in New Mexico.

General lawlessness in New Mexico during the years shortly before and after the Victorio campaign contributed significantly to the problems of the Army and of law enforcement officers, and undoubtedly they influenced the Indians. Indians living on reservations had been victimized by corrupt officials in Washington, as well as by those officials who were less than honest in New Mexico. Some government men who had daily dealings with Indians really did not care what happened to the government's wards so long as they were out of sight and off the land coveted by whites. In addition, outlawry was a serious problem all through New Mexico, for this was the era of William Bonney (Billy the Kid) and others less famous surviving outside the law. Cattlemen and businessmen, as well, operated on the fringes of the law, thereby creating another bad example for the Apaches. As a result of rivalries between competitive economic factions in Lincoln County, an area through which Victorio and other Indians sometimes traveled, a minor war between whites developed.[18]

The Lincoln County War actually began about 1876, but it did not escalate into serious shooting until two years later. It started as a conflict between newcomers and established residents of the county. Lawrence G. Murphy, a rancher, businessman, and master manipulator of money, had lived in Lincoln County for several years, and by 1874 he completely dominated the economic life of the area. He owned the largest cattle ranch, the transportation system, and the general supply stores; everyone had to patronize his businesses if they were to remain in the county. Naturally, Murphy had many enemies, one of whom probably was John Chisum, a powerful Texas cattle baron. Chisum may have been instrumental in bringing to Lincoln Alexander McSween, recently of Kansas. McSween, trained as a lawyer and a peace-loving man, wore no guns when he arrived in Lincoln in 1875. He quickly became involved in the filing of law suits against members of the Murphy faction. The law business improved rapidly, and, probably with the backing of John Chisum, McSween entered into other forms of business directly in competition with Murphy. Increasing his influence was the fact that Murphy apparently had most of the territorial officials on his side. It was said that he loaned money even to Territorial Governor Sam Axtell.

Minor skirmishes, barroom fights, and an occasional wounding of a member of one or the other faction occurred between 1876 and 1878. Then, on February 8, 1878, intense armed warfare erupted. John H.

Tunstall, a cattleman and a member of McSween's faction, was killed by a group alleged to be Murphy's men. Riding with Tunstall at the time was William Bonney, a friend of McSween's. Bonney survived the shoot-out that claimed Tunstall's life, and with McSween he swore vengeance on Murphy. Considerable killing followed in the next several months. Sheriffs, deputies, innocent civilians, and armed ranchers were ambushed in broad daylight, as each side sought revenge. The showdown came during July 16–19, in a wild battle called the Lincoln County War. McSween and a few of his followers were in his home when some of the Murphy faction set it aflame. Shooting started immediately, and when the killing stopped all but two of McSween's men had been shot. William Bonney also survived this affray.

Lincoln County was almost denuded of people, as everyone who could afford to leave packed their belongings and moved out. In September 1878, after receiving numerous complaints about Governor Axtell, Washington officials responded by appointing a new territorial Governor, Lew Wallace. Wallace was little more effective than Axtell, perhaps because he was more interested in his literary career than in solving New Mexico's problems. He was writing *Ben Hur,* and he had hoped for a better assignment, one where he could sit quietly and write. He was not a vigorous leader; in fact, his handling of the Lincoln County War shows why Victorio and other Apaches assumed they could do what they wished in the territory.[19]

Wallace did not arrive in Lincoln until September 1879, and until then he contented himself with calling for amnesty for the participants. He asked for military intervention and martial law, but as the Army had its hands fully occupied, what with Indians, border riffraff, and outlaws, the government refused Wallace's request. Wallace did interview William Bonney—probably more out of personal curiosity than from any real desire to stop the bloodshed in Lincoln. Nevertheless, as a result of the amnesty proclamation, people came forward to discuss their differences, and eventually the conflicts were settled.

Local wars and corruption were not peculiar to New Mexico. Rather, the Territory mirrored the general situation in Washington.

This was an era of governmental scandals right in the Grant administration itself. Undoubtedly, the Indians recognized that they had little
chance to get fair treatment from a people who tolerated corruption in
the high chancelleries of government and allowed activities such as
those in Lincoln County to continue.

In addition to the problems of outlaws, regional wars, the occasional entry into the reservation by the Army, in pursuit of a raiding
party, and dishonest Indian agents, there was also the increasingly
serious and omnipresent problem of the shortage of supplies for Indians who wished to live peaceably. In 1876 the government decided
that the Indians at Ojo Caliente would be removed permanently to San
Carlos. Agent John Clum, in April 1877, was given authority to effect the plan. Clum and his Indian police arrived at Ojo Caliente on
April 20, 1877, prepared to cooperate with Colonel Edward Hatch in
moving those Apaches who were at Ojo Caliente to San Carlos. Clum
took Geronimo's gun and confiscated weapons from other Indians.
Several Indians were away raiding south of the reservation, and the
Army sent units to hunt them down. Clum recorded that conditions on
the reservation had deteriorated because of a weak Indian agent there.
Clum said that the agent knew the reservation was being used as a
point of re-supply and rest for many groups of renegades, but that the
agent had no interest in the matter.

The agent had sent an employee to the Ojo Caliente reservation, in
advance of the main party, to ascertain conditions. When Clum arrived
at the agency, his scout informed him of the hostile attitude of the Indians. Clum vowed to challenge that attitude, and the next morning he
assembled the Indians. Victorio was the chief of the band, but Geronimo and other leaders were also present. Clum had the leaders arrested
and then threatened the tribe if any trouble occurred. He told them that
if they believed they must fight, he would oblige them. They need not
wear out their moccasins looking for him, for he could easily be
found—well-armed and prepared for confrontation.

Clum paused for effect; Victorio then insisted that his people had
been misrepresented, for they were good Indians who only wished to

Apache Indians in line, waiting for their rations, Fort San Carlos, Ariz., 1880. *Western His tory Collections, University of Oklahoma Library.*

live peaceful lives. The agent reminded the chief that even at that moment bands of Apaches were on raids in New Mexico and Arizona, and in Mexico. Furthermore, Clum told the entire band that they would be punished if they left the San Carlos reservation to raid, and he advised them that each day they must report for roll call to be counted as "men" and not "sheep." Clum's appeal and open threat prompted 434 Indians to arrive at the reservation before sunset on April 21. For the next few days Clum's police controlled the Apaches, and except for two days when some "bootleg booze" was given to a few warriors, all was serene. For six days Indians submitted to Clum's counting procedure, and then a potentially dangerous incident occurred.

Clum's usual attire at Ojo Caliente almost cost him his life. He generally wore "a broad brimmed hat, double breasted blue flannel shirt, pants and boots—the pants tucked into the boot-tops, a belt with cartridges, a hunting-knife and a Colt's 'Forty-five,' and a rifle which was carried in a short sling looped over the pommel of the saddle." [20] However, on this day, his gun belt feeling rather heavy, Clum laid his weapons aside just as the Indians were assembling for the seventh day.

On arriving at the agency office, he looked outside and saw a problem brewing in the counting of heads. Forgetting to pick up his weapons, he ran out onto the field, where he found a young Indian sitting on the ground, refusing to get in line. Clum ordered his police

Indian Agent John P. Clum and Apache Indians at Washington, D.C., 1876. Eskiminzin is seated at extreme left of Agent Clum. Clum is at center. *National Archives.*

49

to arrest the man and place him in the guardhouse. The man walked a few feet and then broke away, returning to his original place. Clum seized a rifle from one of the policemen and forced the young warrior to his feet. After walking a few steps in the direction of the guard-house, the captive wrestled free, pulled a concealed knife from his belt, and attacked Clum. The agent later said it was fortunate he did not have his weapons, for he surely would have killed the warriors, creating an ugly incident. Instead, Clum had time only to swing the rifle, delivering a stunning blow to the Indian's head. The incident ended with little damage, and the rebellious brave was placed in irons.

On May 1, 1877, 453 Indians were started on the pilgrimage to Arizona. Guarded by Army troops and Clum's police from San Carlos, the Indians were driven toward their new home. Their weapons taken from them, these new arrivals at San Carlos soon learned just how much they would dislike Arizona. Clum resigned in July of 1877 and H. L. Hart was appointed, contributing to the continued confusion of Indian affairs.

The Indians at last were confined. They had been removed from southern New Mexico. Responsible for keeping them away from their former homes and preventing their raids was the United States Army.

3

THE
INDIAN-FIGHTING ARMY

Lieutenant Henry O. Flipper had been in the saddle now for three tor-
turous days. His eyes were red from the blowing sand and from loss of
sleep, his lips were dry and cracked, and he was almost totally exhausted. Yet he could not stop. Indians had attacked a stage coach four
days earlier, killing the driver and mutilating the passengers. At dawn
the next day the United States Cavalry had been ordered to find and
punish the "renegades." Lieutenant Flipper was an officer much like
other officers, but he also was black. His men were soldiers in the
Ninth Cavalry, and they too were like other soldiers; yet they too were
black—fierce fighting men whom the Indians called "buffalo soldiers." To these black soldiers fell the arduous task of returning hostile Apaches to their reservations. Only marginally members of the society for which they were fighting, these soldiers were used on
assignments against yet another minority. Thus the conflict of cultures—Indian and white—involved still another conflict: black and
red. The black troops were to be the instruments by which sufficient
distance would be put between Indians and whites.

The post-Civil War Army assigned to fight the Indians and police
the frontier was comprised entirely of volunteers. The officers were
usually professional military men, and many of the enlisted men were

Academic Board of U.S. Military Academy, West Point, N.Y., with Colonel Wesley Merritt at center, behind desk. *National Archives.*

seeking either adventure, security, anonymity, social mobility, or survival in a new country. The officers were generally graduates of the United States Military Academy, while most of the enlisted personnel were illiterates who had never had an opportunity for education. Most of the records kept by the participants in the Indian wars were those the officers left; the enlisted men could barely write. The average age of an enlisted recruit was twenty-three at first enlistment and thirty-two at re-enlistment. Recent immigrants to the United States made up a large portion of the enlisted men, for the Army offered these Germans, Irish, Danish, and French hopefuls at least some kind of future. Others who enlisted were men who had progressed up the economic ladder but had gone broke during the Panic of 1873. Still others were blacks, those from the South seeking to escape the turmoil of Reconstruction,[1] those from the North looking for dignity and opportunity.

Some of those who came to serve on the frontier had been soldiers in the West; they were fleeing the boredom and routine of regular Army life. These men hoped for excitement. Many of them had originally enlisted for the money. The pay, although low, was often better than what could be made in civilian life, especially after the Panic of 1873. Army pay and life was even more attractive to blacks than to whites, for blacks had few opportunities to improve their standard of living in civilian life. One sergeant, a young black from Washington,

Line of black soldiers—the "buffalo soldiers"—at Fort Bayard, N.M., *c.* 1880. *National Archives.*

D.C., enlisted in 1880 to see the wild West he had heard about. He also knew that the best government jobs went to veterans, and he hoped that, after his discharge he could use his service career to rise, socially and economically, in the civilian world. Then, too, the Indian-fighting Army attracted ex-Confederate enlisted men and officers, men who often served under assumed names. The Indian wars also offered opportunities for shady profit, and thus the Army in the West attracted a number of petty criminals, and even some hardened ones. Under an alias, before the age of fingerprints, a wanted man could serve his entire life in the frontier Army with little chance of his real identity being exposed. Still, because of the type of enlistee, the low pay, the harsh discipline, and the undesirable duty stations, the ranks were generally under strength during this period. Recruiting was a serious problem, although there were regular recruiting stations in most large cities. At times the Army employed dubious means to persuade men to enlist in the ranks. Buying drinks, paying gambling debts, saving a man from a hanging—these were some of the services performed at times to secure additional manpower.

Although there was no real spirit of militarism in the United States between 1865 and 1890, and no patriotic reason to join the Army, there was always the lure of the uniform. Men, women, and children all seemed to respect the men in blue. This was especially true after the death of George A. Custer in 1876. The "belles" were infatuated by the dashing, daring "yellowlegs," as cavalrymen sometimes were called. However, there were civilians who disliked the garrisoning of soldiers in their area. Public opinion was against having these men close by, where they could date local girls and frequent local bars—and, too, often, brawl with local toughs. Many civilians believed that all soldiers were lazy, good-for-nothing riffraff who should be kept isolated from polite society. When potential recruits learned of such treatment, they were sometimes deterred from recruiting.

The new recruit was supposed to be in good health, able to communicate in the English language, and, the Army hoped, literate. However, in time of need, almost anyone able to walk into a recruiting office was enlisted. After the Panic of 1873, the number of men entering the Army increased so rapidly that recruiting officers claimed they were turning down four out of every five of the would-be volunteers.

Several posts in the United States operated as receiving bases for the recruits. Once enlisted, cavalry recruits were sent to Jefferson Barracks, Missouri; infantry volunteers to David's Island, New York, or Columbus Barracks, Ohio, or, until the early 1870's, to Newport Barracks, Kentucky. At these stations the recruits were processed, assigned to work on fatigue details, and introduced to the drudgery and discipline of the Army. Career non-commissioned officers were usually in charge of the men, and these hard-boiled veterans of the Civil War often used their power and influence to intimidate, cheat, and terrorize green recruits. Most of the supplies were Civil War surplus, making life for the recruit even more uncomfortable.

There was no formal military training at the receiving stations. In fact, the Army did not accept the idea that a man needed to be trained before assignment to the frontier. Until 1884, the Army issued each recruit a copy of the *Soldier's Handbook,* which gave him basic information and advice.

The flavorless Army food consisted of salt pork, dried beans, brown sugar, green coffee, and practically everything that could be made from flour—the last often rather sour and full of weevils. The recruit had no opportunity to obtain better food, for even when rare investigations of the recruit depots were made, no improvement was visible. Breakfast was as unappetizing as the other meals were; it consisted of fried mush, the omnipresent salt pork, or a thin stew that had cooked all night. These same ingredients were frequently combined into an unidentifiable stew—which even the animals refused; yet this dish usually dominated the dinner menu.

Living conditions at the receiving stations were also less than desirable, for the recruit was assigned living space in a large barracks, in which he had only a bunk and a wooden foot locker. Absolutely no privacy existed. There were frequent fights among the recruits, as men's tempers flared over disagreements about card games, wagers, or far less serious disputes. The only activity planned for the recruit at the receiving barracks was the work detail—a chore totally unrelated to the military training he should have been receiving. Occasionally, the men were herded into groups and ordered to perform mass exercises to keep fit. The recruit quickly become aware of Army discipline; at the receiving station he was taught that the military would not tolerate any failure to follow orders.

When the time came for the recruit to be sent to a regular unit, he frequently was marched to his new post. Some new cavalrymen walked several hundred miles to their assignment, herded by an officer and a few noncommissioned officers, all riding horses. It was not uncommon for these new soldiers to march fifteen miles a day, and to maintain that pace for 600 miles. When at last the recruit arrived at his assigned post, he learned yet more of Army life and discipline. Once assigned to a unit, he would more than likely never be transferred out of it. The soldier's first loyalty would be given to his unit—his company was his life. The trooper's only companions were those of his own company; usually the men of one company did not associate with those of another.

Nor did enlisted men associate with officers, for the Articles of War, Army regulations, and specific orders issued periodically enforced the idea that within the Army there were inferior and superior personnel. Officers seldom spoke to privates, except in the line of duty; when an officer gave an order, it usually passed down through the chain of command to the noncommissioned officers, who then conveyed the order to the enlisted ranks. This adherence to rank manifested itself at social affairs at a military post as well, for at gatherings the officers' wives and those of the enlisted men seldom were seen together, and their children did not attend the same classes, if there were any held on the post. Moreover, the caste system was far more rigid during the years of the Indian wars than it had been during the Civil War.

Almost as deadly as the tracking of Indians through the mountainous terrain of the desert Southwest, the Dakota hills, or the Plains country was the loneliness, boredom, and monotony of the Army camp. Forts were usually located on the fringes of settlements, and the men had few opportunities to enjoy the benefits of a near-by town. Generally, they drilled, pulled guard duty, occasionally fought, and cleaned their weapons, a very dull existence.

Army weapons were then a subject of ridicule, at least as far as well-armed outlaws and even some Indians were concerned, for in the first four years following the Civil War, the Indian-fighting Army used supplies left over from the war. Breech-loading rifles were introduced during these years, but seldom did the troops have sufficient ammunition to practice with them. Moreover, the new and effective Gatling guns were curiosities to the men; few soldiers were qualified to operate them. No target practice was allowed, for the cost of the ammunition was extremely high. (One officer in the Seventh Cavalry who wanted his men to practice with the gun was told that if he authorized target shooting, he would have to pay for the ammunition.)

The soldiers' health was generally good at most frontier posts, although at several forts it was necessary to plant gardens and otherwise supplement the Army diet to prevent the outbreak of scurvy and other maladies caused by incorrect diet. The worst problem was venereal disease. All forms of this dread illness ran through the rank and file at the frontier posts. Usually the men contracted the disease from "lower class" Indian women or from prostitutes who lived near the Army camps. Other diseases—diptheria, typhoid, cholera—also periodically menaced the men. Doctors were not in great supply, and the post surgeons, as they were called, did not take the complaints of the men seriously. One enlisted man had a rheumatic ailment, but by the time the doctor and his immediate superior realized how sick he was, he had to be confined to bed for five months. The treatments prescribed were usually primitive; iodine, alchohol, quinine, castor oil, Blue Mass pills, morphine. Dysentery was the most serious of the less deadly diseases, especially to soldiers out in the field. In the Geronimo campaign, one enlisted man who stepped off his horse at night to relieve himself became separated from his company. When he was again ready to travel, he realized he was lost. After several narrow escapes from Indians and considerable fear for his future, he finally reunited with his unit.[2]

Discipline was a major problem, first because it was considered the only training needed to make a soldier tough, and, second, because it was synonymous with punishment. The most frequent cause for discipline within the army was drunkenness. Isolated, bored beyond belief, and generally rather despondent, the soldiers often drank to forget their plight. Another problem was wildness. When stationed near a frontier town, the soldiers were doubtless influenced by the lawlessness and wild life they witnessed. Discipline at a military post varied according to the commander's attitudes. Sometimes hardened noncommissioned officers were allowed to exact exceedingly brutal punishments. Generally, however, official disciplinary action was administered by the officers of the company. According to the reports of some enlisted men, this discipline was often unfair, for a man was generally considered guilty until proven innocent. In some situations, a soldier who was to be court-martialed was held incommunicado for as many as sixty days. He was denied the right to formally appointed counsel, and his freedom to exercise the rights given him by the *Army Manual* depended on the officer in charge of the proceedings.

Murder, robbery, fighting, and insubordination of all kinds were crimes for which a soldier could be brought to trial, but desertion was the most serious crime for which a man was likely to be tried. The officers in command decided what constituted desertion; if a man were absent for only one day from his post, he might be termed a deserter. Secretary of War Stephen B. Elkins said that one-third of all men recruited between 1867 and 1891 had deserted their posts. When caught as a deserter, a soldier might be put in a pit in the ground that was barely large enough to move around in. If he were fortunate, he would be given speedy trial, but if not, he might suffer for days in such a "hell hole," as these were called. Deserters lost their pension rights of course, but that was minor punishment compared to being flogged and sentenced to hard labor, two punishments meted out in the years directly preceding the Civil War.

Often the convicted deserter was branded on the left hip with a letter D, one and one-half inches high. After serving his sentence, he returned to civilian life. However, his record went with him, a permanent sign of his worthlessness. A bad military record limited a man's opportunities in civilian life so seriously that many deserters either went across the continent to unsettled areas or changed their names. During the period from 1869 until the final demise of the frontier, the size of the entire Army was limited by law to a maximum strength of 25,000 men. Most of these soldiers spent more than one-half of their time marching and countermarching in Indian campaigns. Thus the Army was spread so thinly, over so vast an area, that its task was almost impossible.

During the Victorio campaign there were several cavalry and infantry units, but the two cavalry units given the greatest responsibility for the daily chasing and fighting that characterized the Indian wars on the Southwestern Frontier were the Ninth and Tenth Cavalry—the buffalo soldiers. And when Victorio and his band of Ojo Caliente Apaches jumped the reservation to begin their trail of destruction in 1877, the task of containing and returning them again fell for the most part to the Ninth and Tenth Cavalry.

These were not the first black troops to fight for the United States. During the Revolutionary War and the Civil War, blacks had rallied to the colors. In 1861 they had not been welcomed into the Union armies, but as the second year of the war began and casualties mounted, many whites favored black participation. Black troops fought well in many subsequent battles to save the Union. Still, a great many, perhaps a majority, of the white officers refused to command black troops, or accepted the task reluctantly.[3]

At the end of the Civil War, with the hostile Indian tribes of the Central Plains and Southwest ravaging settlements and travelers, the regular Army was reduced in size, equipped with surplus Civil War supplies, and ordered to halt the depredations. In July 1866 Congress passed an act authorizing the United States Army to combine a number of all-black units to help relegate the Indians to the reservations. In August of that year the Ninth and Tenth Cavalry were created, and Colonel Edward Hatch, a native of Maine, became commander of the

Colonel Edward Hatch. *National Archives.*

Ninth. Hatch had entered the Army in 1861 as a captain of the Second Iowa Cavalry and was breveted a major general in 1864 for his gallant and meritorious service in Tennessee. When the war ended he was reduced to the rank of colonel, and in July 1866 he assumed command of the Ninth Cavalry. Blond and blue-eyed, Hatch was a capable soldier who received President Grant's personal endorsement. Significantly, Hatch enjoyed commanding black troops, and, more significantly, he was not a graduate of the Academy, having risen through the ranks to command.[4] The commander of the Tenth Cavalry, Colonel Benjamin H. Grierson, was a native of Illinois. He also was white. Like Hatch, he had joined the Army in 1861. He had served during the Civil War in the Sixth Cavalry. From the rank of major of the Sixth Cavalry, he rose to brevet brigadier general and, later was made major general of volunteers because of his distinguished service. He was assigned as colonel commanding of the Tenth Cavalry in July 1866. Tall, dark, and scar-faced as the result of a childhood accident, Grierson would have preferred an assignment in the infantry. However, he had had experience as a cavalryman in the Civil War; at the request of General Grant he had led a raid through Mississippi, thereby contributing considerably to the victory at Vicksburg.*[5]

Benjamin Grierson did not mind commanding black troops during the campaigns against hostile Indians, but he did object to the places where he was stationed. In 1875, while at Fort Concho, Texas, he wrote his wife and told her of his displeasure with the assignment; he said that if he had to remain in the Department of Texas indefinitely, he would resign from the Army. Grierson was not a professional soldier; he had been trained on the field of battle and found himself an outsider among officers who had been graduated from West Point. He had no desire to be a dashing, daredevil cavalry leader; moreover, he did not

---

* Because Hatch and Grierson were brevetted major general and brigadier general, respectively, as a result of their Civil War service, they were frequently given the courtesy title of "General" by the newspapers and other periodicals of the 1870's. However, both men held the permanent rank of colonel, were paid accordingly, and signed their correspondence with that rank. Therefore I have chosen to use the title "Colonel" in references to them.

Colonel Benjamin F. Grierson, Tenth Cavalry. *National Archives.*

believe extermination was the best way to deal with Indians. In this respect he differed greatly from most military men. He believed that if the Indians were treated fairly, most of the difficulties with them would end. As a result of his unothodox views, some of his fellow officers regarded him as a failure.

According to his wife, Grierson was a sensitive man who was fond of his children, played chess and checkers skillfully, and wrote letters in sing-song verse. He tried to obtain promotion through influential friends, but it is said he did this to help obtain justice for the Indians of the Southwest. Grierson respected black troops, recognizing their ability and their willingness to face danger. He became disenchanted with the Army almost as soon as he began to form his command. Facing difficulty in filling his complement of officers, Grierson remarked, so his wife reported, that he believed the Army was assigning only reserve officers to black units, for regulars had sufficient pull to join other units. Most white officers simply refused to serve with black units. It mattered little to them that the promotion cycle was greatly improved for those serving with the black units on the frontier. Several times during the organization of the Tenth Cavalry, Grierson was ready to resign.

Nevertheless, good officers finally did join the black units. Albert P. Morrow was considered an excellent officer. Morrow had entered the Army in 1861 as a sergeant of Pennsylvania infantry. He soon became a member of the Pennsylvania cavalry and in 1862 was commissioned a second lieutenant. He was breveted colonel of volunteers for bravery in battle. In 1866 he was assigned as captain of the Seventh Cavalry, but in March 1867 he transferred, to become a major in the Ninth Cavalry. He remained with the black unit until 1882, when he was promoted to lieutenant colonel and transferred to the Sixth Cavalry. For Morrow, the Ninth Cavalry offered a vehicle for promotion, and he performed well during the Indian campaigns.[6]

There was one black officer in the Tenth Cavalry who asked to be assigned to the Tenth Cavalry and who performed his duties as well as any white officer: Henry O. Flipper. Born into slavery in 1856, he attended Atlanta University for four years, beginning in 1869. Thereafter he was appointed to West Point, where he realized the odds against his success were tremendous, for he was the first black appointed there. His fellow students did not want him there; nevertheless, his instructors and other officers treated him with fairness. He suffered hazing and total isolation for four years and still was graduated in June 1877.

His request for assignment to a black Cavalry unit was honored, and he was assigned to Benjamin F. Grierson's Tenth Cavalry, then stationed at Fort Sill, Indian Territory.[7]

Black enlisted recruits were easy to obtain. As privates in the United States Army, black troopers received $13 a month, as well as uniforms, horses, and food. There were few places where they could spend their monthly pay, and therefore, just as other enlistees had done for many years, some of them began losing their monthly income by playing cards, rolling dice, or betting on foot races and other games. If the blacks in their soldiering performed below expectations at times, so too did the whites, for the Army Quartermaster Depart-

View of barracks and corrals at Fort Davis, Tex., *c.* 1880's. *National Archives.*

Commanding officer's quarters, Fort Davis, Tex., 1875. *National Archives.*

ment invariably sent them inferior equipment. Worn-out horses and mules, worthless guns, and outdated ammunition made the black soldier's job even more difficult than it should have been.

In 1867, the men of the Ninth Cavalry arrived at Fort Davis and Fort Stockton. They were to patrol the Texas border regions. Apache and other tribes had attacked the settlements, torn down telegraph wires, wrecked railroads, and made travel in this section of West Texas unsafe. Fort Davis, established in 1854, was located alongside Limpia Creek, at a mile-high elevation. The post was named for Jefferson C. Davis, Secretary of War at that time. During the Civil War the post was used briefly by Confederate troops; then it was abandoned until 1867. It was almost totally in ruins when the Army returned; thereafter it was continually occupied until 1891. The first to arrive at Fort Davis in 1867 were the buffalo soldiers, members of the Ninth Cavalry.[8]

During this era the soldiers at Fort Davis were assigned to protect

Officers' row, Fort Davis, Tex., *c.* 1890's. *National Archives.*

white travelers along the El Paso-to-San Antonio road. They were occupied with patrols, escort duty, and campaigns against attacking Indians. Troops from the fort were stationed at key positions, such
places as Van Horn's Wells and Eagle Springs, where they guarded
mail stations. The Army food at Fort Davis was as it had been since
the 1850's: the meat ration was three-tenths bacon and seven-tenths
fresh beef. Bread was made in the post bakery, and it was always accompanied by beans. Until 1869 scurvy occasionally ravaged the men at
Fort Davis; then, at the suggestion of the post surgeon, a garden was
planted. Black troopers were less critical than whites of daily food; in
fact, they generally ate their entire ration. Sanitation at Fort Davis was
not always satisfactory, and dysentery periodically limited troop effectiveness.

Days were long and hot, and entertainment in far western Texas was
scarce. The soldiers whiled away their off-duty hours gambling, drink-

ing, and indulging in the pleasures of the brothels of nearby Chihuahua, a small village populated mostly by Mexicans. Fighting often occurred, and it was not uncommon for a man to die of a stomach
pain—caused by a bullet. Officers were likewise plagued with boredom at the forts in Texas. It once was reported that an officer died of
excessive "inflammation of the stomach"—he drank himself to death.
Life at Fort Davis was typical of that in the frontier posts of West
Texas and New Mexico.

The Tenth Cavalry would eventually be transferred to Fort Davis,
but in 1867 it was assigned to the Indian Territory. Colonel Grierson
initially led segments of his partially organized Tenth Cavalry to Fort
Gibson, while the remainder of the regiment continued to organize in
Kansas. Trouble with Indians on the Kansas borders and the disruptive
attacks of nomadic warriors on the civilized tribes in Indian Territory
kept the Tenth occupied. Before the end of 1869, every member of the
Tenth Cavalry was on duty in Indian Territory. Despite the severe
hardships of hard winters and intensely hot summers, poor food, living

Fort Sill, Indian Territory (now Oklahoma), prior to 1905. Geronimo spent his
last days here. *Western History Collections, University of Oklahoma Library.*

in the saddle for weeks at a time, and under constant pressure from hostile Indians, the black units inflicted considerable punishment on their enemy. Late in 1869, the Tenth Cavalry was ordered to establish headquarters at Camp Wichita in the Wichita Mountains, and for the next six years it suppressed hundreds of Indian raids. Some men deserted, others died, and still others were slowly worn down by disease and exhaustion; in fact, by the end of 1870, Grierson had only about 500 effectives. Three hundred recruits arrived soon after that, but the training program he then faced made his task even more difficult.

In 1873 Grierson was sent to St. Louis to be superintendent of the mounted recruiting service. His successor, Lieutenant Colonel Davidson, was a strict disciplinarian whose actions disrupted and angered the officers of Grierson's staff. Then, in April and May of 1873, segments of the Tenth were transferred to forts in Texas, where they suffered from the hatred of people who formerly had owned slaves. Texans looked upon the blacks with disdain, and fighting frequently occurred between the citizens of Texas towns and the buffalo soldiers.

Along with the Ninth Cavalry, which had been stationed in West Texas along the Rio Grande since 1867, the Tenth Cavalry fought, suffered, and died to make the border regions safe for civilization. Hundreds of miles of brush, mountains, and desert regions, Mescalero Apaches north and south of the border, Kickapoos raiding along the frontier, and the revolution then taking place in Mexico all combined to make the task of these black troopers one of unbelievable magnitude. Moreover, renegades, traders doing business illegally with the Indians, and other border scoundrels continued to wreak havoc on both sides of the international border. When the soldiers arrived at Forts Davis and Stockton in 1867, they found the buildings partially destroyed, and therefore much of their early duty was spent in rebuilding. However, because of the need for constant patrols, the work moved ahead very slowly.[9]

At first, when the black troopers went on patrol, they could not find the elusive hostiles. They had no experience at tracking. Not until the end of 1867 did the buffalo soldiers face the Indians in a major battle.

Nine hundred Indians attacked troopers bivouacking at the site of old Fort Lancaster, about seventy miles east of Fort Stockton, near the Mexican border. Three hours later, after the blacks had killed at least twenty Indians and wounded yet more, the fight ended. The soldiers had three men missing and presumed dead, yet they had accounted themselves well; it was even reported that they had enjoyed the fight. This pitched battle caused the hostiles to be more cautious when facing the Army in close-quarter fighting.

Yet raids continued throughout the region. To counter this increasing pressure, Hatch eventually moved companies to Fort Quitman, under the aggressive Major Albert P. Morrow. Hatch's men were then closer to the areas where trouble was occurring. However, there were few immediate benefits to this change. And, except for a short time when Lieutenant Colonel Wesley Merritt replaced Colonel Hatch, who was sent to Louisiana to participate in the activities of the Freedman's Bureau, Hatch remained in command of the black troopers. During 1868, Merritt did all he could to control the Apaches, but he had limited success. Although the Ninth Cavalry became a seasoned, hardened, and effective fighting force, the raiders learned to strike quickly and then flee to the mountains of Mexico, where the American soldiers could not pursue them. Emboldened by success, the hostiles ranged widely throughout West Texas, striking eastward to Fort McKavett on the San Saba River and to Fort Concho near present-day San Angelo, Texas. The Army doggedly followed; on one occasion Captain Henry Carroll and ninety-five men remained on their trail for forty-two days, marching more than 600 miles. Late in 1869 Colonel Hatch returned from Louisiana and again faced the problem of the increasing Indian raids. The troops' horses and mules had practically collapsed, many of the men were barefoot, their clothing was in tatters, and they were beset by dysentery and other maladies.

Although the hostiles were under greater pressure as a result of the persistence of the officers and men of the Ninth Cavalry, raids continued almost unabated. The Indians frustrated the Army at every turn. Yet the men continued mapping, pursuing, and scouting the mountains

General Wesley Merritt, Commander at Fort Davis, Tex. *National Archives.*

and plains of the region. In many instances, the Ninth and Tenth Cavalry helped the Twenty-fourth and Twenty-fifth Infantry, also all-black
units which had been organized for frontier duty. By the end of 1871,
the experienced Ninth Cavalry had spent nearly five years fighting on

the frontier. Many of the men had not seen their homes since enlisting. Their duty stations were almost totally isolated from civilization, discipline had been severe, and violent death was readily at hand. Receiving little justice and almost no recognition, these men had remained on duty. If they were unfortunate enough to be court-martialed for any reason, they could expect—and would receive—little mercy. Still, with all the hardships, morale was high during this fighting; while the frontier was being tamed, the desertion rate in black units was the lowest in the entire Army.

These black troops suffered even more as the 1870's progressed, for the Mexican government practiced an inconsistent Indian policy. Most Mexican border states were sanctuaries for the Indians, while West Texas was in a state of chaos. In 1870 General C. C. Augur, commander of the Department of Texas, made several changes involving the black Ninth Cavalry. The bulk of the unit would work closely with the black Twenty-fourth and Twenty-fifth Infantry, patrolling along the Rio Grande. From the mouth of the river to just south of the Red River, these units were to scout a vast, 1400-mile arc. In April 1872, the units from Fort Stockton finally reached their designated patrol area. Once all units were on station, their duty was a constant cycle of tracking Indians—usually after a raid—and following them to the Mexican border, where pursuit was supposed to stop. However, Mexican revolutionaries crossed into the United States occasionally, and more than once Cavalry units had to skirmish briefly with these troops. From 1872 to 1876, Colonel Hatch's Ninth Cavalry, aided at times by parts of other units, chased thieves, revolutionaries, and hostile Indians along and on both sides of the international border. No matter how diligent the troops were, however, they could not be everywhere. In addition, when patrolling near towns, the effectiveness of the units was limited because many people did not like soldiers in the vicinity— especially black soldiers.[10]

In 1875 Brigadier General E. O. C. Ord replaced Augur as commander of the District of Texas. It was Ord who commanded the area when Victorio began his raiding along the Mexican border. Although

Major General E. O. C. Ord, U.S. Army Commander, Department of Texas.
Western History Collections, University of Oklahoma Library.

Ord tried to get cooperation from Mexican citizens along the border, they refused to inform the Americans of the whereabouts of bandits, revolutionaries, and, sometimes, even hostile Indians. That same year, Colonel Benjamin H. Grierson, who had been on detached duty, resumed command of the Tenth Cavalry in West Texas. In April, General Ord took additional steps to curtail Indian depredations: West Texas was formed into the District of the Pecos, headquartered at Fort Concho, and Colonel Grierson was placed in charge of the area. Grierson's troops were garrisoned at several posts and mail stations. Assisting Grierson at Fort Davis were three companies of the Twenty-fifth Infantry. Grierson soon learned that companies of the Tenth had been spread all over West Texas. In 1874 these troops had been engaged in the Red River War against the Comanches; they had not been given time or supplies to prepare for further duty in the barren lands of West Texas. Still they continued to do what they could to stop border raids and ravaging.

In the spring of 1876, after repeated efforts to obtain official permission to cross the Mexican border in pursuit of hostiles had failed, Ord's superiors ordered him to use his discretion in observing the international line. Thus, the Indians, who previously had been able to relax in safety across the border, learned that they would no longer have a secure sanctuary.[11] However, the problems of the Army were many, and the fact that the Mexicans did not like buffalo soldiers chasing hostiles in Mexico remained a significant handicap. The Mexican military, although organized to stop Indian raids, was kept busy controlling the activities of internal revolutionaries.

During 1877–78, along the San Antonio–El Paso road, Mescalero and other hostiles attacked isolated settlements and wagon trains. During the spring of 1878, Indian attacks flared violently along the Rio Grande, and unofficial sources reported that fourteen people had been killed in the district as a result. Grierson concentrated his troops in the area, but he had only one man for every 120 square miles.[12] The only tactic available was to keep troops in the field constantly, and this Grierson did during the remaining months of 1878 and 1879. With almost no rest, often with inadequate supplies, and operating understrength, the Ninth and Tenth Cavalry patrolled, chased, and fought Indians and other lawbreakers in West Texas, New Mexico, and Mexico. When Victorio and his Ojo Caliente Apaches left the reservation in August 1879, vowing to fight to the death, the black Ninth and Tenth Cavalry were pressed into even more difficult service. For more than a year, Colonel Hatch and companies of the Ninth Cavalry pursued Victorio almost constantly. Colonel Benjamin Grierson's men patrolled the Rio Grande, thereby forming a wall to stop Apaches from entering Texas.

Yet, for their efforts in the war that followed, black soldiers would be given little credit; rather, they would be characterized as lazy and somewhat dense individuals, while officers such as Hatch and Morrow would often be harshly criticized.

4
THE FIRST OUTBREAK

Victorio, the Ojo Caliente Apache war chief, and Sitting Bull, the Hunkpapa Sioux medicine man and chief, had little in common, except that both were Indian and both led tribes fighting against the United States Army. However, when the warriors of these two tribes performed extremely well against the soldiers, both Victorio and Sitting Bull were categorized as white or part white, for neither Mexicans nor Americans could accept the idea that an Indian could out-general a white man. Shortly after the Battle of the Little Big Horn, when the Sioux fled to Canada, stories began to circulate in the United States that Sitting Bull actually was white, a graduate of West Point, and a Catholic; in 1878 a book, *The Works of Sitting Bull*, was published, ascribing Latin and French poems to his authorship.

Victorio never became as famous as Sitting Bull, which perhaps explains why legend did not transform him into a white scholar and author. However, the stories told about him did ascribe to him a white father. Manuel Romero later swore that his *"padrino"* [godfather], who had fought in the army of Joaquín Terrazas, a rancher, against the Ojo Caliente Apaches, had learned the true story of Victorio's origins. According to this account, an Apache chief named Halcon Negro was accustomed to raiding from New Mexico south into Chihuahua. On one of these forays, the Apaches captured a young Mexican lad named Lardizabal, the son of a laborer on the Rancho del Carmen, which was owned by Luis Terrazas. The boy was taken north and, as was the custom among the Apaches, raised as one of them. As he approached his seventeenth birthday, he was told he could become a member of the tribe and a warrior if he could pass certain tests; moreover, if he performed these satisfactorily, he was to be given as a wife the daughter of one of the great Apache chiefs.

Lardizabal's first test was to perform a war dance in a room whose floor was covered with sharp knives. The other tests were equally severe. However, the lad suffered all the pain, performed well, became a warrior in the tribe, and married the young princess. A few weeks later, when the lad went on his first raid into Mexico, he deserted to rejoin white civilization, leaving a pregnant bride behind. The child later born was named Victorio and grew to manhood hating all whites because he had been abandoned by his father.[1]

Such fanciful legends tell the student of history several things: that Victorio became sufficiently famous to merit speculation about his origins; that the whites often fabricated stories about great Indian chiefs, in part to convince themselves of white superiority and in part to reassure themselves that these leaders were human and not invincible; and, most important, that few real facts are known about Victorio's early life. He was born about 1820; in the late 1870s eyewitnesses described him as approximately sixty years of age. It is possible that he was not born into the Ojo Caliente tribe—he may have been a Mimbres, a Mescalero, a Chiricahua, or even a member of one of the other subtribes. These groups were matrilineal; when a warrior married he usually did so outside his immediate group and then joined his wife's people. Victorio, if not born a member of the Ojo Caliente, probably married into the tribe and thus became a member.

After achieving the status of warrior, Victorio rose steadily. After Mangas Coloradas was killed (1863), Cuchillo Negro briefly exercised control over the tribe. But Victorio quickly emerged as the true leader. He was a great tactician in battle—according to some admirers, the

Victorio, Ojo Caliente Apache chief. *National Archives.*

greatest in the history of the Southwest. His followers were extremely
devoted to him; in fact, members of the tribe allegedly threatened on
one occasion to save their leader from the whites by killing him and
eating his flesh so that the soldiers would not have the privilege of
capturing him. Despite his ferocity and sagacity in battle, however,
Victorio always claimed his true love was peace; until his death he insisted that if only the United States would fulfill its treaty obligations

and let his tribe live on its own reservation at Ojo Caliente, New Mexico, he and his warriors would abandon the warpath.

Unfortunately, he was not allowed to remain in New Mexico. On March 20, 1877, Agent John Clum received orders from the Commissioner of Indian Affairs to move the Ojo Caliente Apaches from New Mexico to the San Carlos Reservation in Arizona. There they would be quartered with several other Apache sub-tribes, including the Chiricahuas. Clum coordinated the actions of his Indian police and Apache volunteers with the movement of troops from the Ninth Cavalry and arrived at Ojo Caliente on April 21. Victorio and members of his tribe protested having to abandon their half-ripened gardens and their livestock. Some of the warriors slipped away into the mountains as renegades—only to see their women and children, along with their aged, marched away to the west. Pionsenay, a Chiricahua Apache, became the most notorious of the renegades who refused to go to San Carlos; he remained free, raiding in New Mexico and fleeing into Mexico for protection—where he also ravaged the countryside.

Meanwhile, those Ojo Caliente Apaches who had gone peacefully with Clum arrived at San Carlos on May 20. There Clum tried to incorporate them into his system of reservation government, which included Apache police, judges, and juries. However, Victorio and his followers resisted integration, insisting that their only desire was to live in peace in New Mexico and that the government had broken its treaty with them by forcing this move. That summer at San Carlos proved difficult for the newcomers. Food was scarce, and the other tribes there were for the most part old enemies. John Clum, who honestly intended them no harm, resigned effective July 1, 1877; moreover, the success of renegade tribal members tempted those who initially had not resisted to flee.

H. L. Hart, the agent who succeeded Clum, proved unable to handle the situation. Hart was a tactful man who tried to reconcile Apache and Army antagonisms. He allowed Army inspection of Indian camps; and although Indians then living within reservations were not subjected to this inspection, the constant civil-military struggle, failure to

receive supplies, and petty tribal jealousies kept the Ojo Calientes dissatisfied. Seemingly, the tribe awaited an opportunity for an outbreak.
During the night of September 1, 1877, Pionsenay, the renegade Chiricahua chief, returned to the reservation to secret away noncombatants
of his tribe; despite all of Hart's efforts, Victorio and Loco, leading 310
members of the Ojo Caliente Apaches—women, children, and the
aged—fled the reservation and headed for the mountains.[2]

The moment Victorio and his people left San Carlos, they were no
longer of concern to the local Indian agent or to the Bureau of Indian
Affairs; rather, they were a problem for the Army, whose task it was
to harry them and induce them to surrender and return to the reservation. Lieutenant Charles B. Gatewood, a young officer who would
come to know the Apaches well, even to speak their language, commented in 1877, shortly after his arrival, that the hostiles at San Carlos
were restless for good reason. They had been robbed by local whites
and by other Indians, they had been abused by corrupt and incompetent agents, and they had been confined despite the fact that as natural
nomads they detested confinement. Gatewood, a twenty-four-year-old
Virginian and graduate of West Point who was serving with the Sixth
Cavalry, was no idealist about the Apaches, however; he noted that
Victorio's followers had an innate desire to raid, and that on such
forays they were given to theft, pillaging, and murder. He stated that it
was part of the socio-economic system of these Apaches to create
havoc among their neighbors, and that their general attitude was
summed up in the word "revenge."

When Victorio fled San Carlos in 1877, Lieutenant Gatewood was of
the opinion that the hostiles would be easy to track, for they had left a
trail through the Territory and south into Mexico, one marked by
"burned ranches, forest fires, dead cattle and sheep, and the bodies of
murdered human beings." Even so, he said, "It is scarcely surprising
that they could not be overtaken by troops that had to use the same
stock week after week, and could seldom follow the trail at night." [3]
Yet it was not Gatewood and the Sixth Cavalry that had to track these
renegades. Rather, the task of returning the Apaches to San Carlos fell

Lieutenant Charles B. Gatewood, Sixth Cavalry, with Indian scouts. *National Archives.*

largely upon the officers and men of the Ninth and Tenth Cavalry, the black buffalo soldiers.

When the 310 men, women, and children following Victorio fled from San Carlos, New Mexicans feared that the hostiles would take refuge in the mountain ranges in the western part of the Territory. Arizonans, within whose boundary the San Carlos reservation actually lay, were also worried; they feared that the renegades would remain in their own area, to prey on local citizens. The Indian police at San Carlos almost immediately took the trail of the hostiles, departing the day after the outbreak. They finally caught Victorio and his followers near the Natanes Mountains; in fact, they trapped the hostiles against a sheer wall of one mountain. As always with these Apaches, they were prepared for the assault that followed—it was virtually impossible to surprise them. In the fighting the Indian police captured the horses and mules that the renegades had stolen when they departed San Carlos, but they were unable to capitalize on their advantage and recapture the Apaches. The hostiles somehow escaped, slipping away through the pursuers' lines.

The chase thereupon commenced anew. For several days Victorio and the hostiles sought to lose their pursuers in the mountains. Near Ash Creek another engagement was fought, a bloody affair in which some of Victorio's warriors were killed and thirty women and children were captured. However, the wily Apache leader led most of his weary band to safety; to the trackers it seemed that the hostiles simply disappeared north of Ash Creek (south of Fort Wingate). Critics of the Apache police would later assert that this escape could not have occurred without their knowledge, while their defenders would point to the battle of Ash Creek as evidence of their loyalty and their fighting spirit.

Victorio knew that he would find no sanctuary in these mountains and arroyos, although this was a region he knew well. Moreover, he desperately needed additional horses and mules, for he and his warriors either had lost their own animals or had worn down the remainder. Therefore, these Apache hostiles raided several near-by ranches, killing twelve settlers and stealing some 100 animals. They also foraged for food and supplies during this campaign against the local citizens, constantly moving to avoid the pursuing police from San Carlos and detachments of army troops in the vicinity. Several battles took place, skirmishes in which the Indians fared worse than the soldiers and local militia. The Indians knew that their situation was desperate, and they fought hard; they believed that surrender to the soldiers meant they would be taken to Florida for imprisonment, as other hostiles had been—and that they would be shot if they fell into the hands of the irate civilian volunteers out hunting them.

New Mexico Territory (present-day New Mexico and Arizona) and the western corner of Texas. Hunting grounds of the Apache tribes. ⸺⟶

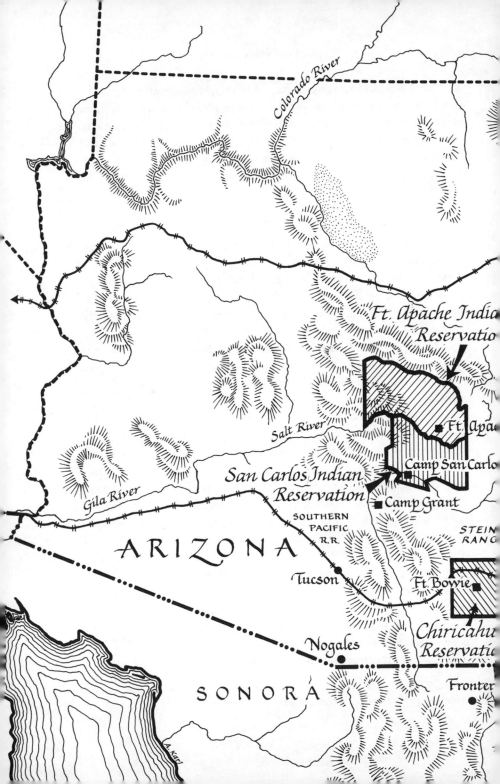

During this run for freedom, fifty-six of the Indians were killed or mortally wounded, and, finally, Victorio decided he had no choice but to surrender. Therefore, he and his 190 starving and discouraged followers came to Fort Wingate. Later, an additional fifty would surrender there—after the Army agreed to let the tribe return to its ancient homeland at Ojo Caliente. Such was the promise of Colonel Edward Hatch, commander of the District of New Mexico. This decision was one of rare good sense, since the return to Ojo Caliente had been the major goal of these Apaches from the start. Hatch told them that they could live there as long as they remained at peace, neither attacking settlers in the New Mexico nor molesting travelers passing through the territory. Hatch had no authority to take this action, but he did so from his personal conviction that this was the only way to keep the Ojo Caliente Apaches on the reservation and off the warpath.[4]

Once at Ojo Caliente, however, Victorio was unable to control his young men. As always, the warriors followed their own whims. Any man among them could organize a raiding party, and those who wished to would join him. Slipping away from the reservation, they would fade into the countryside, strike their target, and then reappear at the reservation. Most of the raids that occurred at this time were conducted in the Mexican state of Chihuahua, not in New Mexico, indicating that even the young men realized that they would be returned to San Carlos if they broke the peace near Ojo Caliente.

In Chihuahua, government officials were becoming more and more exasperated by these raids. Although plagued by local revolutionary activities and unable to devote full attention to the Indian problem, these officials vowed to undertake a sustained campaign to end the Apaches' attacks; the object of this campaign would be to free the state of what was called a "social plague." As leader of this campaign, the authorities appointed the distinguished Joaquín Terrazas as colonel of militia. Terrazas was a seasoned campaigner who had fought both Indians and revolutionaries across the years, and he had distinguished himself on many occasions by his ferocity in battles against hostile Indians. He had learned better than anyone in official position—almost as well as the natives themselves—his way among the mountains and deserts of Chihuahua; he knew how to survive the heat of the deserts and where to find water when others were dying of thirst. The local citizens had confidence in him, claiming that some caravans of wagons had been saved from destruction merely by speaking his name. Here was a man to gather followers, to track the Indians, and to bring peace at last to the troubled state.

In late 1878 and early 1879, Terrazas patiently began the reorganization of the militia forces of the state. He encouraged the local ranchers to become regional chieftains, an excellent plan for these *hacendados*. Each knew his own region well; the mountains, deserts, and plains near by were their homes, and they could compete with the Indians there. This new approach was not tested in the spring of 1879, however, for at that time the hostiles reportedly told Mexican officials they would return to the United States and not bother Chihuahuans again. Once the renegades departed, the Mexicans no longer were concerned with them. Let the hated *gringos* and their own Army contend with Victorio.[5]

Yet the American Army was hampered by a vacillating policy on the part of national officials. Functionaries from the Bureau of Indian Affairs could not formulate a definite policy for the Apaches. Simultaneously, two other Apache chiefs at the San Carlos Reservation, Juh and Nolgee, began attacking travelers in the vicinity; soldiers were sent to catch and return them. At last Generals Philip Sheridan and William Tecumseh Sherman threatened to withdraw the soldiers from southern New Mexico and Arizona and to allow Victorio to roam the countryside at will. This threat at last produced unity on the part of Bureau officials: all Apaches were to be returned to San Carlos and there taught to be farmers.

Captain F. T. Bennett of the Ninth Cavalry was given the assignment to move the Ojo Caliente Apaches back to San Carlos. With two companies of troops, and guided by Apache Scouts, Bennett arrived at Ojo Caliente on October 8, 1878, and informed Victorio of the decision. The response was immediate: Victorio, a few braves, and eighty women and children fled into the mountains, preferring the hunted life of hunger and discomfort to the slow death of the spirit at San Carlos. Seventeen more Indians later joined them. The soldiers began the pursuit anew—merely taking up where they had left off the year before. Meanwhile, the remaining Ojo Caliente Apaches, 169 of them, were taken by Captain Bennett to Fort Apache, where they arrived in December.

Through the mysterious means of communication between Apaches on and off the reservation, Victorio learned the fate of the rest of his people. He knew they would be safe at Fort Apache during the winter of 1878–79, and he chose to wait until spring. During that winter food was scarce in the mountains, and he and his renegade followers suffered severely from hunger and from the ravages of disease and exposure; by spring only twenty-two of them were yet alive—and they knew they could hold out no longer. In February they surrendered at Ojo Caliente, only to cause consternation among the local officials. Colonel Hatch refused to remove Victorio and his small band without specific instructions from Washington, while local Indian agents argued that the renegades should be sent westward at once.

While the bureaucratic wheels ground slowly toward a decision, Victorio had heard yet another rumor—that he and his people were to be transferred to the Mescalero Apache Reservation at Tularosa, New Mexico. He wanted no part of that reservation either, for when the Ojo Caliente Apaches had been there previously they had been assigned to an isolated, almost inaccessible canyon. Moreover, the agent who had worked with them before, Frederick C. Godfroy, by treaty obligation should have supplied them with foodstuffs, including flour, sugar, salt, and other necessities, but he had not stood by the treaty. The Indians had not always received the supplies regularly, and what they did get often was of such poor quality as to be almost inedible. Only by killing the deer that ran wild in the area were the Indians able to keep their women and children from starving. Perhaps what made this situation so intolerable to the Indians were the cattle grazing on their reservation land, cattle belonging to near-by white ranchers who had moved their animals illegally onto Indian lands.[6]

For these reasons, Victorio, for the third time in just a few short months, fled the reservation at Ojo Caliente in April 1879. Word of the outbreak spread quickly, even into Chihuahua. General Geronimo Treviño, who commanded the Mexican forces along the international boundary with the United States, journeyed to Mexico City to present his plans for controlling the frontier. He told his superiors that he and General E. O. C. Ord, commanding the American troops in Texas, had completed an agreement concerning difficulties along the Rio Grande and proposed reciprocal border crossings, sharing of information, and concentrated American-Mexican action.[7]

American officials likewise hoped to cope with the situation, especially agents in the Bureau of Indian Affairs. They wanted some solution that did not involve the Army. Therefore, S. A. Russell was appointed the agent to the Mescalero Reservation with instructions to bring peace to the region. A quick study there revealed to Russell why the Ojo Caliente Apaches had fled into the mountains rather than move to Tularosa. However, he proved incapable of standing up to the ranchers and local suppliers.

While Russell and a few concerned individuals searched for a solution that did not involve fighting the whites at Tularosa, Victorio and his followers remained off the reservation, dodging pursuit by the Army. Through the mountains, the semi-desert region, and the rolling plains of the area the hostiles rode, raided, and sought sanctuary. Colonel Wesley Merritt had brought a company of cavalry to Ojo Caliente late in April; he hoped to stop the Indians before raids began in earnest.[8] Troops also were moving toward Ojo Caliente from other directions; Company "E" of the Ninth Cavalry passed through Albuquerque early in May under the command of Captain Ambrose E. Hooker. According to New Mexican observers, these troops appeared capable of giving Victorio considerable trouble.

Major Albert P. Morrow had his command of the Ninth Cavalry

also looking for the hostiles. Victorio and his followers were believed to be in the San Mateo Mountains. Despite this pursuit, raids and plundering continued throughout southwestern New Mexico. All available units were in the field, and one company of cavalry was posted at Fort Cummings, given twenty days' supply of rations, and told to scout the country north and south of that point. Morrow took "G" Company of the Ninth Cavalry across the mountains to join other troops converging on the area. It was expected that Morrow would catch Victorio during this chase.[9]

New Mexicans suffered through yet more Indian raids during May 1879, and with increasing frequency other Apaches were emboldened by news of their brothers' successes; they slipped away from the San Carlos Reservation in Arizona to raid in southwestern New Mexico. The cavalry was constantly in the field searching for the Indians. Finally, late in May, one military unit discovered the hostiles. Captain Charles D. Beyer and Lieutenant Henry H. Wright brought their men up quickly. The renegades outnumbered the troops by three to one, and for a few moments it seemed that they would rout the soldiers. However, after a considerable exchange of rifle fire, a determined cavalry charge caused the hostiles to break and run in every direction.

Returning to the command posts, the soldiers reported one trooper killed, two wounded, and several horses shot from under the hard-charging cavalrymen. Rumor placed the Indian losses at about fourteen wounded, some of whom, possibly, were dead; but, more significantly, all the Indians' horses and supplies had been captured. Yet, even after this defeat, the hostiles were able to get away into the San Mateo Mountains. The embarrassed Army, with Colonel Edward Hatch commanding the District of New Mexico, was determined again to stop the raids, but could do no more than continue the dreary schedule of patrols and tracking that previously had occupied most of their time.[10]

The renegades may have raided rather widely in Texas during this period, for Army units stationed at Fort Concho reported recapturing nineteen of the horses the Indians had stolen earlier. Some newspaper editors conjectured that the hostiles perpetrating these attacks were part of Victorio's band from New Mexico.[11] On June 30, 1879, Victorio and his weary, bedraggled group appeared before an Indian agent and agreed to go peaceably to the Mescalero Reservation. Thus, until September, they would be under Army control.

However, even while they were on the reservation, raids continued to occur throughout the summer. In Arizona, New Mexico, and Texas, hostiles attacked isolated ranches and settlements. In July, a group of unidentified Indians raided a ranch in Limpia Canyon, just three miles east of Fort Davis; a woman was killed in this raid and sixteen horses were stolen. A contingent of civilians and soldiers from Fort Davis pursued the attackers toward New Mexico—far enough to prove the hostiles were from some reservation. It was believed these Indians were Apaches from the Fort Stanton Reservation.[12]

Indeed, by this time Victorio's band had again left the reservation. In July, a civil indictment had been brought against Victorio at Silver City, New Mexico, charging him with murder and horse stealing. Some Apaches might have been guilty of such lawlessness, but in the midst of the intense turmoil it was an unwise civilian reaction. Late that summer, a New Mexico judge and a hunting party rode through the Mescalero reservation. Victorio heard rumors of his impending arrest, and when he learned of the arrival of the judge and his party on the reservation he took flight again. Actually, by this time the Apaches had decided they could not remain on the Mescalero Reservation. On September 4, 1879, Victorio and his band pledged each other they would fight to the end. They would not be trapped again by soldiers, nor would they ever surrender. There were other—and significant—reasons why the Indians left Tularosa, for Victorio and his followers had been on the Mescalero Reservation only a short time when trouble began with Indian Agent S. A. Russell. As a result of Agent Russell's inability or unwillingness to supply Victorio's band with adequate supplies, and the natural animosity of Apache factions toward each other, there was little chance for harmony.

Immediately after escaping from Tularosa, the Victorio band traveled toward the San Andres Mountains, then crossed the Rio Grande and sought sanctuary in the Black Range. These mountains were so rough that literally thousands of arroyos, valleys, and other hiding places were available to them. Moreover, this was a beautiful area, with ample game, water, firewood, and cool mountain air. Women, children, and older men rested there for several weeks while the warriors moved through the region foraging for supplies. The group remained ready for flight if discovered, and each night careful preparations were made for an expected Army attack.

In September 1879, Victorio raided the soldiers stationed at Ojo Caliente, stealing their horses. To hinder pursuit, he stationed braves along the ridge of the canyon through which the pursuers had to ride. These wily warriors pushed large stones down on the troops, discouraging effective pursuit. Moreover, the Army had insufficient mounts to pursue for any great distance. For almost a week the Apaches disappeared, apparently into thin air. Then the cavalry was ambushed on the Rio Percha, and Colonel Dudley's men suffered losses. To further disguise their whereabouts, the Indians led the Army toward the Big Bend country of Texas, away from the tribe's favorite haunts in the Black Range. They also fled from one range to another, confusing the cavalry.

Undoubtedly this was a hard life, but the Apaches preferred running to being quartered at San Carlos or at the Mescalero Reservation. At times during these chases, the hostiles would ride into Mexico; there Victorio could get ammunition and supplies in return for giving the villages protection. Still, some Mexican villagers tried to lure the Apaches to their death by offering them mescal, getting them drunk, and then massacring them. Victorio forbade his tribe to drink the fiery Mexican liquor; instead he allowed them occasionally to drink their native beer, *tiswin*.

Late in 1879 and early 1880, while the Indians were in Mexico, American authorities estimated that Victorio had several hundred warriors. In truth, however, the Apache leader had only about seventy-five, and there were never more than 450 people in his group at any time. A few

Mescaleros and Lipans, less than fifty, did at times ride with Victorio.

Citizens throughout the Southwest continued to criticize the government for allowing reservation Indians to raid and then return to reservation sanctuaries. In fact, Texans at one point claimed that they had followed raiders "to the very doors of the agent of that [Fort Stanton] reservation, but no effort was made by that official to secure the thieves; in fact, he discouraged the officers in their pursuit." They argued that if the government would make more of an effort, the problem could be solved. Many Texans thoroughly believed that there was "something rotten" in the administration of Indian affairs, and that the sooner the government recognized the seriousness of the Indian difficulties, the sooner a solution could be found. Indians had attacked Texans in order to obtain supplies, and the citizens insisted that "if Texas has to supply these Indians, we would like to have the state get the benefit of the appropriation for that purpose." [13]

New Mexican citizens living directly in the raiders' path were extremely anxious to see military action taken against Victorio; particularly in Las Cruces, the people tired of the deeds of "the marauding and murdering" Indians. They argued that at no time had General Hatch been given the authority "to offer immunity to thieves and assassins." They denounced the Army's actions, saying that the soldiers scouting for Victorio could easily have killed or captured him, "but it seems considerably cheaper to sue for peace with him and reward him for his crimes than to punish him." [14]

Likewise, the citizens at Las Cruces distrusted Agent Russell. This Mescalero agent insisted that the Indians under his jurisdiction were innocent of most charges levied against them. Russell referred to the reports of citizens as "editorials" of the newspaper *Thirty-Four*. Caustically, the editor remarked that Agent Russell obviously knew "fully as much about the Indians on the Mescalero reservation as he does about English grammar. . . ." [15]

On September 17, 1879, after Victorio's band had fled the reservation, New Mexican Governor Lew Wallace reported the Indian depredations to the United States government and requested that the Secretary of

91

War permit the New Mexicans to recruit three or four companies of volunteers to chase Victorio and punish him for the "horrible atrocities committed on the citizens." [16] William W. McCrary answered the Governor the next day, telling him that the Secretary could not authorize such actions, but that he would arrange for troops to be concentrated in the southwestern section of New Mexico.[17]

Governor Wallace replied that seven whites had been killed in a fight with Indians near McEvers Ranch, fifteen miles from Hillsboro. This had occurred on September 11, 1879, and on that same day ten Mexicans—men, women, and children—were also murdered, about three miles away. Apparently the hostiles had committed atrocities, torturing their victims, for the bodies had been horribly mutilated. Moreover, in this same attack twenty-five women and children had been badly wounded. Although no one knew for certain that this fierce and sanguinary attack was perpetrated by Victorio, he was blamed. The Indians were said to be well mounted—probably on the horses stolen in the attack on the cavalry that took place shortly after the Indians left the reservation. Significantly, the newspaper in Las Cruces delayed by several hours publication of its September 17 issue in order to include descriptions of the attack and letters from Hillsboro asking for help.[18]

The exchange of letters between officials was not yet over, for on September 18, 1879, the Adjutant General's office wrote to General John Pope, who commanded the Department of Missouri, explaining that since the Secretary of War could not give Governor Wallace permission to recruit militiamen in New Mexico, the office would like to know the plans of the military to cope with the most recent outbreak.[19] Pope replied to the Adjutant's office that all available troops had been in pursuit since early September and that everything was well in hand. He did relate that, although Captain Hooker had lost ten men in a brief battle with hostiles, there were ample troops to bring the Indians under control. John Pope had been graduated from the United States Military Academy in 1838. He had served gallantly in the Civil War, in which he had been a major general. He was a brigadier general at the time of

Nana, 1884. *Western History Collections, University of Oklahoma Library.*

the Victorio outbreak and had succeeded General Philip Sheridan as commander of the Department of Missouri.[20]

Pope gathered the information readily available to him, and on September 18 he reported to the Adjutant General's office the details of the Victorio outbreak that had taken place earlier that month. According to Pope, Captain Ambrose Hooker's men, guarding the horse herd, had been attacked on September 4 by a group of Apaches led by Victorio and Nana. The Indians had killed five soldiers and three civilians guarding the herd, and had captured a number of military animals. He estimated that as many as forty Indians had taken part in the attack.[21] In response to this attack, all available troops had chased the Apaches. Major A. P. Morrow, temporarily in command at Fort Bayard in southern New Mexico, sent his troops scouring the countryside for the wily Apaches. By the end of September, as raids on civilians increased, it was rumored that Victorio had about seventy-five men, and that his success had brought him additional recruits from Mexico. Realizing how difficult it was to track the hostiles, the Army immediately assigned Lieutenant Charles B. Gatewood, with fifteen troops and twenty Indian scouts, to watch for Apaches who might approach San Carlos from New Mexico, seeking contact with their families.

Actually, Victorio and his band had traveled into Arizona, hoping to find sanctuary there. The Army officials in Arizona responded by organizing expeditions throughout the Southwest to track the renegades. At Camp Huachuca, Arizona, Lieutenant Guy Howard and Company "D" of the Indian scouts, with a detachment of Sixth Cavalry, searched the area east of the camp. Lieutenant Augustus P. Blocksom and a detachment of Company "C" of the scouts were sent into the field from Fort Bowie, while Captain Tullius C. Tupper was sent from Fort Grant to patrol the surrounding hills, and General Eugene A. Carr left Fort Lowell, at Tucson, to take command of the entire Sixth Cavalry. Thus the Army employed a strategy it would use many times: immediate screening of the area to control and capture the Apaches.

However, Victorio and his band, in a move unknown to the Army, crossed back into New Mexico about September 18. Shortly thereafter, Captain Byron Dawson, with a detachment of forty-six Navajo scouts

Captive Apaches at Fort Bowie, Ariz., in 1886, after surrender. The woman at the far left is covering her sliced-off nose—the Apache punishment for adultery. *Western History Collections, University of Oklahoma Library.*

Fort Bowie, Ariz., 1885. Photo taken by Lieutenant Gatewood. *Western History Collections, University of Oklahoma Library.*

and men from the Ninth Cavalry, stumbled on Victorio's trail. Furthermore, Dawson and his men had the misfortune to be the troops closest to the new-found trail, at the head of the Sierra Blanca Canyon. They began immediate pursuit. Lieutenant Gatewood later wrote that he had a low opinion of the Navajo scouts and suggested that, when compared to Apache scouts, the Navajos "belonged rather to the coffee-cooling class, and, with several exceptions, made serious objections to following a trail that was getting warm." [22] Nevertheless, the Navajos led the cavalry directly after the Apaches, and, unfortunately, directly into a clever ambush.

In fact, the trail was about five days old, but it was easily followed, for it was marked along the way with bloody rags, the remains of butchered cattle, and the graves of dead Indians. Early on the morning of September 17, at the head of the Las Animas, the scouts realized the hostiles were nearby. The path led up an almost inaccessible hill, which the scouts began to climb with their carbines at the ready. About 150 yards from the top of the hill, a single shot killed one of the Navajo scouts. Bedlam broke loose immediately, as a withering crossfire rained on Dawson's men. The soldiers were pinned down, unable either to escape or to attack. [23]

Despite their predicament, Dawson and his men returned the fire at Victorio and his Indians—there were approximately 150 of them—who had laid the ambush. With no way out of the trap, Dawson and his men abandoned their horses, sent for help, and sought what little shelter they could find. They knew it would take several hours for any help to arrive. Before the Army could respond with any strength, fifty-two troops from Hillsboro, under Captain Charles D. Beyer, mostly militiamen, were seen approaching through an arroyo. With these reinforcements, the Army was able to continue the fighting all day. Word of the battle was sent to Major Morrow, who ordered Lieutenants Blocksom and Gatewood to the area. Gatewood and Blocksom had been at Fort Bayard only a short time when they received Major Morrow's orders. Scouts with detachments of cavalry under Lieutenant Blocksom went straight across the Mimbres Mountains to the scene of

Barracks building, with soldiers at attention, Fort Bayard, N.M., *c.* 1880's. *National Archives.*

the fight, and the rest of the cavalry followed the wagon road that passed near Fort Cummings, hoping to encircle the hostiles.[24] Gatewood recorded that it took several days to climb through the Mimbres, for there was no trail to follow and the mountains were "tough and precipitous." Gatewood, although not a participant, later said that the men who had fought had performed bravely under the accurate hostile fire and in the face of death. Lieutenant M. W. Day of the Ninth Cavalry, for instance, had, during the heat of the battle, refused an order to retreat and leave his wounded on the battlefield. He personally carried a disabled soldier away under heavy rifle fire, and his commanding officer, Captain Beyer, wanted to have him court-martialed for the effort. Fortunately, Day was not punished for his heroism; in fact, he later received a gold medal for his bravery. After this fight, Captain Beyer withdrew his weary men forty miles, regrouped, and marched toward Fort Bayard.[25]

Finding the fight over and the hostiles gone, Lieutenant Blocksom's

Gatehouse of Fort Bayard, N.M., *c.* 1880's. *National Archives.*

detachment set out in pursuit. Rumors prevailed late in September that Victorio had been killed or wounded in the Las Animas fight, but they would prove untrue. After this fight ended, the Indians once again slipped away into mountain sanctuaries. The Army had suffered five killed and one wounded, as well as a considerable loss of livestock. One civilian and two Navajo scouts had been killed, bringing the total to eight killed in the skirmish. Moreover, fifty-three horses and mules had been abandoned, while thirty-two of the animals were killed. And a large quantity of baggage, supplies and other paraphernalia had been lost when the horses bolted the area.

After some four days, the Indians' trail was found northwest of Animas Canyon. Leaving their pack mules behind, and accompanied by a few scouts supported by a dismounted detachment of cavalry, Gatewood followed the trail for three nights. During the daylight hours they concealed themselves and rested for the ensuing night's march. It rained almost constantly and the men could not build fires to dry their clothes or to cook food for fear of giving the hostiles information on their location. Equally disconcerting to the soldiers was the fact that their bread, and especially their tobacco, "fell into a pulpy mixture that could neither be eaten nor smoked." [26]

On the third day of the chase, the hungry, tired, but determined soldiers, having the day before eaten dried horse meat, discovered an abandoned government mule that the Indians had overworked and left to die. Gatewood described the appetizing picture: "It was not difficult to see every bone in his body, and his back was a mass of—what you might expect to see on a mule so much abused. From the time his throat was cut by a scout till a stew of bacon and mule was simmering on the little fire in a frying pan picked up on the trail, a very few minutes elapsed." [27] By the end of the third night's march, Gatewood knew for certain that he was on the trail of Victorio; more important, he knew the Apaches were unaware that they were being followed. On the fourth day the scouts were joined by the cavalry, which had been marching to meet them with supplies. Pausing only briefly to fill their saddle packs, the group continued on.

When the rain stopped, the intense sun bore down, searing everything under it so severely that within two days the soldiers again showed signs of exhaustion and collapse. In particular, they needed water. At the end of the fourth day the group traveled during daylight, and scouts stealing silently ahead of the main party soon discovered Victorio and his band camped in a deep canyon. The Indians and the soldiers saw each other at the same time, and spontaneous firing began. The hostiles believed that the scouts were the only soldiers present, and therefore they mistakenly assumed an easy victory. Gatewood reported that the Indians "became quite saucy and facetious, daring them to come closer, and even inviting them to supper." [28] The Indian overconfidence was short-lived, however, for the remainder of the troops, hearing the firing, hurried forward and joined the fight. Wisely, the Indians took advantage of the descending darkness and quickly slipped away. Two dead warriors and a squaw, along with several wounded, were the Indian losses; the Army had suffered no casualties. With the retreat of the hostiles, the scouts and troops bivouacked for the night, the scouts camping about a mile from Major Albert P. Morrow's troopers.

The next morning, just as the scouts were finishing breakfast, pandemonium again broke loose. First a single shot and then more and more volleys, accompanied by shouts of command reverberated down the canyon. Lieutenant Augustus P. Blocksom sent Lieutenant Gatewood with twenty men on foot to report to Major Morrow, but they could not break out. Gatewood later said he thought all the troopers had gone mad, but one corporal surely had kept his bearing in the confusion, advising Gatewood that he was sitting on the wrong side of a rock to be protected from the cross fire, and there was no future in the Lieutenant's trying to protect a rock. Actually, not all the troopers were as disorganized as Gatewood at first believed, for once behind the rock he noticed that many of the men were firing coolly; some were even joking and laughing. Within an hour more scouts arrived from the camp, positioned themselves behind the hostiles, and loosed a deadly barrage into the Indian ranks. The troops were ordered to flank the hostiles, but many of the soldiers were uncertain whether the scouts, too, were in the brush. According to Gatewood, rising above all the noise came the "fog-horn voice of Sergeant Jack Long bellowing forth, 'Mucho Bueno! God d—n come on!' " Gatewood's later account stated that it was "very encouraging to see your enemy trying to break the sprinting record, racing with your bullets." [29]

As the hostiles fled the battle scene, there was no use trying to follow them, for the rocky terrain seemed, as always, to swallow up the Indians. Later, when the soldiers overran the hostiles' former position, they saw pools of blood and bloody rags, evidence that many of the Indians had been wounded. Only three of the Apaches had died in the skirmish. Major Morrow wrote to General Pope on September 24, 1879, giving the official report of the fight that had occurred on the eighteenth. Morrow, acting in Colonel Edward Hatch's temporary absence, indicated that he would personally lead the troops in the field, and that his temporary campaign headquarters would be the McEvers ranch, a centrally located position.

The Army claimed, in official reports to the Secretary of War, that it had "inflicted severe punishment on the Indians." Major Morrow led an attack on the Indian camp and recaptured sixty horses and mules, some of which the hostiles had taken from Hooker during the original outbreak early in September. Several soldiers were killed during these battles, and others were wounded. Neither side could win a decisive victory at this time, however, and the Indians once again broke off hostilities and headed for sanctuary.[30]

Early in October 1879, Morrow reported that his troops once again were tracking the Apaches. According to his reports, the Indians had left the Mimbres Mountains and headed into the Mogollon ranges, hoping for better protection there. In fact, this officer believed that the Indians might be seeking sanctuary in Mexico rather than in the United States.

In Texas, there was strong criticism of the Army at this time for allowing the hostiles to escape. Editors raged in their papers, while civilians wrote hot letters to their Congressmen; all complained of the disturbances, destruction, and death left in the wake of the Apaches. The Texas frontier, from Fort Davis to El Paso and south to the Mexican border, was almost constantly harassed by these and other Indians. Texas newspapers carried daily news stories of Indian depredations. The Indians were the public enemies of Texas, and accordingly, the Texans were critical of any restrictions on the pursuit of them into Mexico. According to these citizens, the United States Army had done little to curtail the raiding. Texas had borne the brunt of the onslaught, and since 1874 the state had annually appropriated more than $150,000 for maintaining Rangers in the field against the Indians.[31]

The first problem in capturing the renegades was finding them. Colonel Hatch and his men vigorously searched within the United States, and for weeks at a time could find no trace of the Apaches. Some citizens thereupon took matters into their own hands. Captain O. Crouch organized a party of thirty volunteers from Mesilla and Las Cruces and led them to Colorado, New Mexico, to aid the besieged citizens there. On October 13, 1879, these men found an Indian trail and followed it eighteen miles from Slocum's Ranch. It led them directly into a trap. The volunteers fought desperately, having seen what the Indians had done to their victims at McEvers Ranch. Perhaps 100 Indians participated in the battle. White losses included W. T. Jones, county clerk of Donovan County, and four Mexicans. From Mesilla an additional contingent of two companies, totaling eighty men, was raised and sent to join the pursuit. After reinforcing the citizens fighting at Colorado, New Mexico, the volunteers and military patrolled southwestern New Mexico, helping the besieged people at Varejo and Santa Barbara. The latter village was actually surrounded by hostiles and had asked the Army to come to its rescue.[32]

It mattered little to the settlers in the area whether Victorio or Geronimo, or, for that matter, some other group, committed the atrocities. Governor Lew Wallace of New Mexico related the general feeling about the Apaches when he said they were unquestionably the most troublesome group: "Kindness makes no impression upon them. They too are what they were when the Spaniards found them—cunning, blood-thirsty, and untamable." [33]

On October 16, 1879, General John Pope sent information to General of the Army William Tecumseh Sherman concerning additional Army losses. Although not officially reported in Army records, it appears that Lieutenant Blocksom's scouts may have fought Apaches, probably Victorio, and suffered considerable losses.[34] Seventeen scouts and two enlisted men had died in a skirmish. General Sherman forwarded this information to the War Department, detailing Army strength in New Mexico. Major Morrow had about 500 troops, 100 of whom were Indian scouts. Civilians in the area, as well as Army officers, wanted the government to supply rations for the proposed 500-man civilian militia. In the midst of all this trouble, a squabble began over the appointment of an agent for the San Carlos Agency in Arizona. Army officers urged the War Department to fight any attempt to appoint a civilian official; these officers believed the Army could best handle the situation.

The raids in southwestern New Mexico at this time may have been led by Indians from Mexico, and not by the Victorio band, as the press insisted. In fact, Victorio's band may already have fled the United States, for the Army reported that the last time it had heard of or seen the Apaches they were heading for Mexico, hoping for sanctuary across the border. Government officials had, in fact, advised the Mexican consul at Tucson that the Apaches might attempt to sneak into Mexican territory. The governments of Chihuahua and Sonora had been asked to capture the hostiles if possible. Unfortunately, there was much internal trouble in Mexico—especially along the frontier—and these officials had few resources and little time to fight Indians.

In addition, it was widely known in the United States that the Mexicans in Chihuahua had more than Indian troubles to overcome before they could attain stability and offer safety to the inhabitants of the

Tucson, Ariz., 1880's. *Western History Collections, University of Oklahoma Library.*

state. Returning Americans, even those who had spent only a short time in the state, reported that the country was in serious trouble. Drought had affected the country's crops, Indians were approaching to within a short distance of the major city of Chihuahua, and twice the Indians had defeated the Mexican militia near the capital. And, although Porfirio Díaz was firmly in control in Mexico City, internal revolution reportedly still plagued the frontier. Many people believed that Governor Angel Trías should be overthrown. Trías had his hands tied. During the month of September he had bought 125 Remington carbines at El Paso, but he subsequently found that he could not get them to his soldiers; the loaded caravan, on its return trip to Chihuahua, had been attacked by political opponents, and they had captured all of the rifles and the 80,000 cartridges. Trías could do very little to bring the raiding Indians under control. However, the average citizen of New Mexico and Texas little appreciated these Mexican problems.[35]

While newspapers in the southern sections of the territory were criticizing Colonel Hatch for his failure to find the Apaches, the *Weekly New Mexican* at Santa Fe had a more realistic editorial. On October 4, 1879, the editor of the paper wrote an editorial stating that the real problem with the Indians had been created by the Indian Bureau. "For years these Indians lived contentedly upon their reservations at Ojo Caliente," the editorial read, "and but for the greed and intrigues of a few scheming and unprincipled men would be at peace with the whites now as then." Many new Mexicans agreed.[36]

Colonel Edward Hatch and his command of black troops followed the Indians and vigorously attacked them at every turn. Yet the Indians were so tenacious and fought so gallantly that the Army constantly had to retreat and bring in more troops or await more supplies. Praising Hatch at this date, the editor insisted that he was "a vigorous and efficient District Commander, and has always done everything possible with his handful of men, and we shall be very much mistaken if Victorio does not hear from him in a decided manner as soon as the circumstances will physically admit of it." [37] Others also expressed confidence in Hatch; Governor Sam Axtell of New Mexico said that Hatch

San Francisco Street, Santa Fe, N.M., 1860's. *Western History Collections, University of Oklahoma Library.*

"had been vigilant to prevent outbreaks, and when they have occurred has been prompt to suppress them." [38] Thus, at least early in the Victorio campaign, many people in New Mexico still exhibited faith in Hatch and the Army. That a good deal of this support evaporated within a short time was not entirely Hatch's fault.

Major Morrow had considerable difficulty finding Victorio during October. At one point near the end of the month, Morrow reported that neither he nor Gatewood and his scouts had been able to locate the hostiles. Yet the Indians were still near by, for attacks were being reported during the chase. Morrow then learned that McEver's Ranch had been burned, as had several other ranches in the area. Morrow reported to Ambrose E. Hooker that he had caught up briefly with Vic-

Santa Fe traders, arriving Santa Fe, 1860's. *Western History Collections, University of Oklahoma Library.*

torio and had fought him. In one such skirmish Morrow related that, after dislodging the hostiles and capturing their camp, the Army discovered evidence of several seriously wounded hostiles. Short of water for animals and men, however, Morrow could not pursue the Indians, but had to seek fresh water at Rio Cuchillo Negro. And Indian scouts working for Morrow had captured a number of horses and mules, some of which had been taken from Hooker's command. Morrow insisted that he needed more ammunition and men, but wrote that he would continue the pursuit regardless. The country was almost inaccessible, and Morrow believed that it would take several days of hard fighting to drive the renegades out. He also reported that two of his men had been killed in recent fights. Two days later he learned that Victorio had left the Mimbres and Black Range and probably was heading toward Mexico. Morrow sounded confident that he would be able to stop the Indians with the supplies he expected to receive, but that it would take months to accomplish this task.[39]

Deciding he must follow the hostiles, Morrow allegedly gained temporary permission from Mexican officials to enter Mexico. The Americans hoped to catch up with the hostiles before they went too far into the interior. During Morrow's chase the Army also learned additional and disconcerting news. It was reported that a number of Mescalero Apaches from the reservation near Fort Stanton had joined with Victorio in his raiding. Major Morrow had difficulties keeping up with Victorio, however, and he wrote again to General Pope that he needed some additional equipment. Only if he had two mountain howitzers, fifty pack mules, and other equipment could he hope to keep pace with the quick-moving enemy. He related also that he expected the Indians to recross the border into the United States within the month.[40]

Late in October, Morrow, eighty-one enlisted men, and eighteen Indian scouts followed the fleeing hostiles several miles into Mexico—they marched 115 miles in seventy-nine hours—and when they caught up with them the ensuing fight was not representative of the Army's ability. Fatigued beyond belief, thirsty, hungry, their senses dulled, the officers and men did their best to stop the Indians. Morrow said that the hostiles were abundantly supplied with ammunition and with animals. He related that the Indians had "killed from 600 to 1000 [horses and mules] since the outbreak, when the animal becomes too footsore to go further the Indians shoot him." Concerning the terrain, Morrow related "It is impossible to describe the exceeding roughness of such mountains as the Black Range and the San Mateo. The well-known Modoc lava beds are a lawn compared with them."

The hostiles got the better of the battle, and the fighting ended when the troops decided that without water they would not be able to win the fight. Morrow later insisted that he tried again and again to capture the Indians during this fight. He added that he was "opposed as much by natural obstacles as by the enemy." Likewise he feared wasting his ammunition, so he withdrew to where his horses were picketed. After seeing the condition of his horses and men, both desperately needing water and rest, he ceased chasing the hostiles, hoping for a later opportunity.[41]

Lieutenant Gatewood had been involved in the chase from Palomas Lake, and he aptly described the difficulties of following hostiles into this type of terrain. Marching in the boiling heat by day, the men camped at night always looking for water. Through sand and heat and across deserts and mountains the trail led ever southward. Each horse that tired and fell was shot, thereby placing another cavalryman on foot. At one camp the troops found a pool of mud in an alkali flat, and there they decided to stop for the night. Both men and animals tried to drink the mud-laden alkali water, but got no refreshment from it. Gatewood recalled that "there was no singing, no joking, no conversation, no smoking in the column, and the banjo of a colored soldier that used to enliven the men was silent." [42]

Officers' quarters, Fort Bayard, N.M., an early photograph. *National Archives.*

Animals corralled inside Fort Bayard, N.M. *National Archives.*

The soldiers then came to a tank of cool water, but the Indians had replenished their supply and then had disembowled a coyote and thrown it in the tank, and otherwise poisoned the water. Twenty miles from Janos the trail led between two parallel ridges where the hostiles set an ambush. The scouts detected the trap and warned the soldiers. Gatewood noted:

> Men steadily advanced into a rougher and more broken mountain region. The Indians seemed to have plenty of ammunition and the whole top of the mountain was a fringe of fire flashes. Nearer and nearer to the top of the ridge approached the flashes from our Springfield carbines and the reports from their Winchesters above were so frequent as to be almost a continuous roar.[43]

Thus, wasting no further time, Morrow ordered his men to withdraw.

Gatewood was moved by the reactions of the men, for when they left the area "many men showed symptoms of that wild insanity produced by great thirst." When they saw the water in a small stream "white, colored and red men, horses and mules, all rushed pell-mell for the water. They drank of it, they rolled in it, and they got out of it and returned to it. They wept and cheered and danced in it, and the mud they made seemed to make no difference in drinking." [44] Morrow's command arrived at Fort Bayard on November 3, 1879, and Morrow reported to his superiors.

Thus, the Ninth Cavalry, having chased Victorio a considerable distance into Mexico, was forced to give up pursuit. Permission to cross into Mexico had not, in fact, been given to Major Morrow, and would not be, from Victorio's outbreak in September 1877 until his final demise. Nevertheless, American troops occasionally crossed the international border. Victorio demonstrated in these early outbreaks that he and his people wished to live only at Ojo Caliente, otherwise they would remain off the reservation to raid and cause destruction to border areas. On both sides of the international border, military leaders continued to search for a way to capture the wily Apache, but it would be several months before any lasting success could be attained.

5

CIVILIANS, RANGERS, AND MEXICANS

By the fall of 1879, the ranchers, farmers, and townspeople of New Mexico had become highly vocal in their scorn of the Army and its failure to defeat the Ojo Caliente Apaches and their leader Victorio. Yet few knew or understood the difficulties faced by the Army. Most believed, in part because of the headlines generated by Major Albert P. Morrow's relentless pursuit of the renegades, that as many as 500 soldiers had been assigned to this task; yet at no time were there more than 200 troops in a camp near enough to the hostiles to be effective. Moreover, when soldiers did get close to the Indians, they could never force them into a decisive battle, for the Indians were too familiar with the local geography. As well, their horses were far superior to those used by the Army; the military mounts were huge animals that had to be grain-fed, and were highly irritable in the field, where grain was unavailable. The Indian ponies were accustomed to feeding on grass.

Not only did New Mexican civilians believe that large numbers of soldiers were in the field, but they were also convinced that the Army was receiving real help in the pursuit of the hostiles from Mexican troops and militia, as well as from Texas Rangers and New Mexican volunteers. The Mexican forces in 1879 were inadequate; most of them were irregulars more interested in booty and scalp bounties than in the capture of the renegades. And the New Mexican volunteers were almost as useless. Once, Morrow followed the hostiles up to the Candalaria Mountains, where he had to turn over the pursuit to fifty-two Mexican frontiersmen; he later learned that these volunteers had set out in pursuit—only to discover that they had been led into a trap. In a ten-hour battle, most of these men were killed, proving both that the hostiles were deadly dangerous and that the volunteers were unable to function effectively. The Indians never enjoyed such success against the Army; in fact, they respected the soldiers to the extent that they rarely tried an ambush against them. That they did ambush the civilians proved simultaneously that the Army was worthy of respect and that the volunteers were not.

The Texas Rangers in the field, although they were active and effective in pursuing the hostiles from August 1879 until the end of the cam-

North side of main plaza, San Antonio, Tex., early 1880's. *Western History Collections University of Oklahoma Library.*

Market square, San Antonio, Tex., 1870's. *Western History Collections, University of Oklahoma Library.*

paign in October 1880, never numbered more than twenty. They confined their activities officially to West Texas, although occasionally—and unofficially—they crossed into Mexico when hot on the trail of renegades.

The leader of the Rangers was George W. Baylor. Born in the Indian Territory in 1832, Baylor, who was married and had two daughters, assumed this task in the summer of 1879, moving his family 600 miles westward from San Antonio to the little village of Ysleta, some ten miles down the Rio Grande from the American town of El Paso and the Mexican village of Juárez. By no stretch of the imagination could this have been considered choice duty, but Baylor undertook it, as he did all his assignments, with diligence and ability. He was forty-seven years old at the time, standing six feet, two inches tall, and was impressive in bearing, fearless in the line of duty, and a family man who always treated everyone fairly.[1]

Colonel George W. Baylor, Texas Ranger. *Western History Collections, University of Oklahoma Library.*

Baylor headquartered his Rangers in the town of El Paso, for his orders were to patrol the border in that area. He arrived in the town in September in company with Sergeant James G. Gillett, and soon he had his men in the field and was making their presence known. The following month a note arrived from the Mexican authorities in Chihua-

James B. Gillett, Sergeant of Texas Rangers, 1870's. He traveled with George Baylor into Mexico in search of Victorio. *Western History Collections, University of Oklahoma Library.*

hua; this told of an attack by fifteen Apache renegades on five Mexicans cutting hay. At first it appeared that only one man had survived this attack, but later the authorities learned that all the men had scrambled to safety in the underbrush. The note concluded that the renegade

Apaches were heading toward the Texas border. The Rangers left as soon as possible to track the hostiles. Five miles below La Quadria, near where the attack on the Mexicans had occurred, the Rangers found "sign" that the Indians were not far away. Arriving in the Mexican village of Guadalupe, the Rangers joined with the Mexican militia, which also was searching for the hostiles. The Rangers then traveled to Don Romana Aranda's ranch, arriving there at the same time as did Mexican volunteers from other sections of the state. Twenty-three men, led by local Mexican militia officers, had gathered. Finally, the Rangers and the Mexican allies arrived at the mouth of the Cañada del Marranas, in the Sierra Betanos Mountains of Chihuahua, and there confronted the hostiles.

A major fight began immediately. Sergeant James B. Gillett fired at the hostiles, whose return fire almost cost him his life. Baylor later said that in the bright daylight prevailing he had instructed his men not to fire unless they actually saw an Indian. However, the Rangers fired in the general direction of the flash of the enemy's guns and at the smoke rising from behind rocks. The hostiles soon broke away and the fight ended. The Rangers and Mexicans suffered no losses, but the hostiles lost three men and an undetermined number of wounded.[2]

On this *entrada* into Mexico, as on subsequent missions, Baylor and his men enjoyed friendly relations with Mexican citizens and troops. Baylor even signed an agreement with the *Presidente* of Guadalupe which permitted Mexican troops to cross the border when pursuing the hostiles. Baylor declared that his agreement "informs the Mexicans, with artless simplicity of language, that they can come over and kill all the reservation Indians they can find. . . ."[3]

While in Mexico, Baylor and his command of fourteen Rangers arrived at Carrizal where the fifty-two Mexicans had been ambushed only a few hours after the battle. The Texans were moved by the courage displayed, and Baylor described what he saw in these words: "The scene of the conflict was perfectly horrible. I saw in one little narrow parapet, which the beleagured Mexicans had hastily thrown up, seven men piled up in a space 6×7 feet. The Indians had shown great cunning, as they have through all this campaign." [4] This battle had been a grisly one by any standards. Baylor reported that an additional thirty-five men, seeking to find their fallen comrades, had come down from New Mexico in an attempt to find survivors of the ambush. These brave souls had also fallen into the same trap and had been hard hit; thirty-two men had been killed, while at least another eighteen had been badly hurt. The fight had lasted nearly ten hours and served to warn civilians of the fighting strategy and capability of the Indians. Baylor believed that as many as 200 Indians had taken part in the slaughter. He also surmised that the Apaches again were heading northward, probably back to New Mexico.

Army officials learned, early in January 1880, that the Mexican government in Chihuahua was finally in a position to participate in the campaign against Victorio. The Governor of that Mexican state advised these officers that Generals Geronimo Treviño and Joaquín Terrazas once again had taken the field. On December 20, 1879, General Treviño launched a campaign, taking to the field at the head of some 500 men.

Treviño, like most leaders in Chihuahua, had been born in the state, and during his life had gained considerable experience in dealing with the Apaches on the frontier. He had fought for the liberals in 1858, had resisted French intervention, and, as leader of the "Legion of the North," had won considerable fame as a brave and fierce fighter. Thus he, like the others who would be placed in command of units trying to catch Victorio, was well qualified for the job.

Early in January newly appointed Governor Luis Terrazas, who had succeeded Angel Trías in November, 1879, telegraphed General John Pope, asking him to post troops along the border to intercept the hostiles, who might be recrossing into the United States. Shortly thereafter, Terrazas advised Pope that about 100 hostiles had gone north after committing many acts of depredation in Mexico. [5]

Although Mexican officials at this time said they could handle the Indians, Chihuahua was still suffering the ravages of revolution. The situation was stabilizing itself only slowly. The *pronunciadas* (or revolutionaries) had proclaimed the removal of Governor Angel Trías and had briefly captured Chihuahua City. General Geronimo Treviño, with a large federal force, easily recaptured the city. In sum, the effect of his activity was to remove Trías from power and replace him with the popular Terrazas. Still there was little stability, for while Treviño was trying to reconcile all the political elements, about 300 men, partisans of the *pronunciadas,* captured the town of Guerrero and declared in favor of ex-Governor Trías. In the midst of these disturbances, the Indians' raids continued unabated. Until the fall of 1880, difficulties between state and federal commanders also hindered the fighting of Indians.[6]

Meanwhile, in New Mexico, during late December and early January, Governor Lew Wallace suggested that the returning Indians might head for the Florida Mountains. Therefore, he argued, the cavalry should be prepared for such a move. Newspapers in the territory warned the citizens: "Trouble is brewing. Rumors fill the air. A dozen contradictory reports are afloat with regard to the Indians. Nothing is known as to their whereabouts; but a feeling of uneasiness is manifest on all sides." [7] Major Morrow, Hatch's field commander, was then at Fort Bayard recovering from the fatigues of his last battle with Apaches. He quickly moved men into the Florida Mountains, hoping to block an Apache return.

However, the problem was not only one of defeating the Indians in battle; it also involved changing the hostile attitude of the government, especially that of the many officers who were involved. For example, early in January 1880, Brevet Brigadier General John Pope, commanding the Department of the Missouri, wrote a stinging indictment of the Apaches. He said, "Everybody knows beyond the probability of dispute that the Indians on this reservation (like all the Apaches) are a miserable, brutal race, cruel, deceitful and wholly irreclaimable— although for years they have been fed by the government and 'civilized' by their agent they are in no respect different from what they were when the process began." [8] It is likely that Pope never considered the possibility that no improvement in Indian relations had been achieved because too many people in New Mexico would consider only his assessment of the Apaches.

In January 1880, Edward Hatch, colonel of the Ninth Cavalry and commander of the District of New Mexico, ordered his entire regiment into the southern part of the Territory and took personal command, thereby assuring himself of criticism by the press. Hatch also requested reinforcements from General Orlando B. Wilcox, commander of the Department of Arizona; a number of scouts from the Sixth Cavalry, including Lieutenant Charles B. Gatewood, Major Anson Mills, and Captain Curwen B. McLellan, were sent to scout the west side of the Sierra Mimbres and the Mogollon Mountains. Moreover, Colonel Eugene Carr and the Sixth Cavalry were at Fort Grant, and were ready to cooperate with Hatch or with General Treviño of the Mexican Army.

Colonel Eugene Carr, born in New York, had entered the Army in 1850. He was a captain when the Civil War began. Breveted to the rank of colonel, and later to major general, Carr was a cavalry officer from the beginning of his career. Although mustered out of service in 1866, Carr became lieutenant colonel of the Fourth Cavalry in 1873. He was promoted to colonel of the Sixth Cavalry in 1879, and served in this position during the Victorio campaign. When Carr retired, in 1893, he had served nearly forty years as a cavalry officer. During the Victorio campaign he commanded troops of the Sixth Cavalry, and he was alleged to have looked with disdain upon the black soldiers of the Ninth and Tenth Cavalry. He was known by the Indians as "War Eagle," and he knew it was his duty to assist the black troopers.

Troops from the Ninth Cavalry—119 men in all—left Fort Stanton on January 10, 1880, to scout the Guadalupe Mountains. In Texas, troops from Forts Stockton and Concho patrolled the Llano Estacado area to keep the hostiles from escaping in that direction. Finally, in the belief that all these efforts were insufficient, the legislature of New Mexico passed a bill appropriating $100,000 to provide funds for the Governor to call out 1000 militiamen. Governor Lew Wallace also wired the federal

General Eugene A. Carr, Sixth Cavalry. *National Archives.*

government, asking permission to invite Mexican troops to cross the border when in actual pursuit of the Apaches.[9]

During this same month, thirty Mexican merchants in a pack train owned by Juan Zuloaga arrived in Las Cruces, New Mexico, reporting that they had been with Mexican irregulars in the Florida Mountains, where they were attacked by Apaches. They claimed to have lost eighty mules and $10,000 worth of merchandise and that several of their party had been wounded. These same merchants reported that the volunteer troops had disbanded, but that Mexican regulars were pursuing the Indians toward the Mimbres Mountains. The Mexican troops, however, refused to cross the border into the United States, and the hostiles slipped away.[10]

Hatch immediately ordered Major Morrow into these mountains. Morrow's command consisted of companies "B" under Captain Byron Dawson, "C" under Captain Beyer, and "H" under Captain George Augustus Purington. About fifty Indian scouts also accompanied this detail. Under the command of Lieutenants John T. Wright and James Maney, they struck the hostiles on January 12, 1880, near the headwaters of the Rio Puerco in the Sierra Negrita Range. The battle lasted from two p.m. until sundown, when the hostiles broke away, heading northeast with Morrow pursuing. According to his reports, six Indians were killed, others probably were wounded, and one or two Indian scouts and Sergeant Gross of the Ninth Cavalry were killed. Others had been wounded, but none seriously.

For a week Morrow continued to follow the hostiles north into the San Mateo Mountains. On January 17, the soldiers again caught up with them and another engagement took place. After several hours of fighting, in what was described as terrain of the "roughest possible nature," the Apaches fled yet again. This time it was not possible to ascertain Indian losses because they had an opportunity to conceal their dead in the surrounding country. During the fighting Lieutenant J. Hansel French was killed while leading his men up a steep ravine defended by hostiles. After this skirmish Morrow was out of ammunition and other supplies; therefore he advised the War Department that, as soon as he could obtain needed equipment from Ojo Caliente, he would resume the chase.[11]

Since the Indians still had not been successfully confronted, Hatch decided to organize and keep in the field at all times three different columns: one consisting of Major Morrow's command, another made up of men from some of Morrow's troops stationed at Fort Stanton, and a third comprised of men from several different outfits and commanded by Captain Ambrose E. Hooker. The Army was indeed pressuring the hostiles more effectively; the number of raids reported grew less and less.[12]

On January 23, 1880, Morrow reported he was only two hours behind Victorio. Late that day the troops caught up with the hostiles, but Victorio chose not to fight and he turned southward, seeking sanctuary. Morrow captured more than 100 horses and mules and an immense amount of stolen plunder, which was quickly destroyed. Mariano, the head chief of the Navajo volunteers accompanying this command, offered to lead 100 picked warriors in pursuit of Victorio. The Navajos wanted only ammunition and supplies. Morrow quickly accepted their help.[13]

It mattered little how few or how many scouts followed the Apaches, for during the remainder of the month only minor skirmishes occurred between troops and hostiles. Then, on January 27, 1880, part of Victorio's band attacked a supply train destined for Morrow's command. Forty men of the Ninth Cavalry and about twenty Indian scouts repulsed the attack. Captain Henry Carroll reported that one scout had been killed and two soldiers wounded. Carroll could not leave the train to pursue the hostiles, however, and the Apaches escaped.

On January 30 Morrow divided his command, sending Company "M" of the Ninth Cavalry under Captain Rucker and Company "E" of the same group under Captain Hooker to different areas along the Rio Grande. The main group under Morrow continued to follow the hostile's trail. Hooker and Rucker discovered the Apaches about five miles north of Palomas and immediately attacked them as they were

Major Henry Carroll, Ninth Cavalry, July 1, 1898. *National Archives.*

crossing the river. In this battle yet another Navajo scout died, three cavalrymen were wounded, and a few animals were killed.

During the night of January 31, the hostiles silently crossed the river again and headed up the *Jornada del Muerte* toward Martin's Well. When Morrow arrived at that watering place, he telegraphed Hatch

123

that once again the Army was but a few hours behind the hostiles, and that their trail this time led toward the Mescalero Reservation. Morrow, after advising Hatch of his recent manuevers, marched his men to Aleman's Well, still hoping to overtake the hostiles. At daylight on February 2, 1880, Morrow led his command away from this location.[14]

Meanwhile Hatch had ordered troops from several posts to be placed in the field to try to trap Victorio and his band. Even Governor Terrazas of Chihuahua, who was finally winning firm control of that state, volunteered to have state troops stop the Apaches should they head south.

Morrow's column encountered the hostiles again on February 3, 1880, in an area of lava beds and *malpais* on the east side of the Sierra San Andres and northeast of Aleman's Well, in the San Mateo Mountains. Victorio's band quickly occupied a strong position at the top of the steep bluffs, and the ensuing fight lasted all day. At dusk Morrow and his men gained a foothold and dislodged the enemy, but in the darkness, using the roughness of the country as cover, Victorio and his warriors slipped silently away, heading in a southerly direction. One Navajo scout was killed and four soldiers of the Ninth Cavalry were wounded. Yet there was optimism throughout the ranks, for the soldiers and officers believed that at last they had trapped Victorio. Mexican troops were in position in the Guadalupe Mountains, and other units of the United States Army were in position to ensnare the elusive Apaches. However, fighting that began optimistically again on the morning of February 4, 1880, ended in disillusionment, for the Indians soon broke off the engagement and fled. Morrow's men were far too exhausted to chase the fleeing hostiles.[15]

When Colonel Hatch heard of the difficulties that Morrow and Rucker had encountered, he immediately took the field himself, ordering units southward from Santa Fe. But he was unable to trap the hostiles. Apparently, the Indians were able to slip back and forth through the Army's lines almost at will. Hatch insisted that the Indians were "certainly as strong as any command Major Morrow has had in action. . . . The Indians select mountains for their fighting ground

. . . are thoroughly armed and as an evidence they are abundantly supplied with ammunition. . . ." [16]

These soldiers were not the only ones trailing the Indians during January, for Lieutenant George W. Baylor and his Texas Rangers were almost constantly on patrol in West Texas and Mexico. On January 19, 1880, ten Rangers commanded by Sergeant James B. Gillett rode 100 miles to a stage station at Crow Springs, Texas; they rescued a shepherd dog that alone had held the station for fifteen days. Two mining engineers had been trapped inside. These survivors, more dead than alive, had slipped out of the besieged station, leaving the dog to decoy the attacking Apaches; they had walked 100 miles over extremely

group of typical Texas Rangers, 1882. *Western History Collections, University of Okla-ɔma Library.*

difficult terrain to the Ranger station at Ysleta, arriving on January 18, 1880. Preparing quickly, Gillett and his Rangers made the round-trip rescue to the stage station in a week, found the dog still on guard, and were overjoyed at the opportunity to save the animal. Victorio and his band evidently remained in Mexico only for a few days—if they actually had been there at all during January.

In early February, while the troops and Rangers were occupied with chasing Victorio, Colonel Hatch asked the War Department to consider moving the families of braves living at San Carlos to Ojo Caliente. He assumed that this would facilitate rounding up the renegades, who eventually would come to wherever their loved ones were being held. He also made this request because he and his officers believed that the Mescaleros on the Tularosa Reservation were aiding, abetting, and even at times joining the Victorio band. Therefore, these Army officials wanted to disarm the reservation Indians and to confiscate their horses, hoping that this eventually would have a significant effect on Victorio's mobility. The Secretary of the Interior agreed to the plan, stating that his department recognized that the Mescaleros had no use for guns and horses "except to depredate, as there is but little game in that vicinity; and the best and most economical policy is to compel the Indians to remain upon their reservation and furnish them with sufficient supplies. . . ." [17] However, most of the Indian agents resident in New Mexico opposed this plan.

Late in March more information regarding the removal of Victorio's dependents from San Carlos to Ojo Caliente was sent to the Army command in New Mexico. General Pope cabled General Sherman that to leave "families at San Carlos is simple [sic] to prolong hostilities and be the occasion of unnecessary death of both White men and Indians." [18] Despite these arguments, the Interior Department would not agree; not only were the agents opposed, but also many of the Indians did not wish to be moved.

At about this same time, reports of considerable Indian raids continued to filter through to Colonel Hatch and to the civil authorities at Santa Fe. One rancher complained to acting Governor William G.

Ritch of New Mexico that Indians had attacked his ranch in western New Mexico; although such acts of depredation were not the Governor's responsibility, this Socorro Country rancher asked for guns and aummunition with which to equip and field a small force of volunteers. After all, said the irate rancher, the Army is "encamped in different places where there is no danger of seeing the Indians." The feeling that the Army was incapable of solving the problem was definitely growing.[19]

One citizen, formerly an agent to the Apaches, wrote to the Santa Fe *Weekly New Mexican* that he had had considerable experience in dealing with Victorio and other renegades, and he stated his opinion that government officials had used an incorrect approach in their attempt to bring the Indians to terms. He reminded readers of the newspaper that from the beginning the government had promised the Apaches in New Mexico that they could remain on the Ojo Caliente Reservation. The government had constructed a fine agency at that location, and the Indians when there had caused no one any trouble. Yet, said this former agent, men of short vision living in the eastern sections of the United States had determined the desirability of removing all Apaches to San Carlos, and that had been the start of all the trouble. After their removal to San Carlos, the Ojo Caliente Apaches had waited only until the military left the area and then had fled the reservation, raiding and stealing only what they needed for subsistence. When finally they all regrouped, they went directly to Fort Wingate, surrendered to the Army, and were removed to Ojo Caliente again. During the year that the Apaches had been allowed to remain at Ojo Caliente, no trouble had been noted. Then they were turned over to officials of the Department of the Interior, which had ordered their removal once again to San Carlos. Some Apaches had gone to Arizona, but many had fled to Mexico. This former agent said he later talked with Apache chiefs who promised that if they could live at Ojo Caliente they would cause no trouble. Still, he concluded, there were those in government who insisted on moving the Apaches permanently to San Carlos, and therefore the only recourse for the Ojo Caliente

Apaches was to fight. Only a realistic program satisfactory to all concerned would resolve the dilemma and allow safety and security to reign again in the southwestern border regions.[20]

During that spring of 1880, reports of raids continued to arrive at Army headquarters from all sections of southern New Mexico, but some question existed as to whether or not Victorio and his followers were the perpetrators of these acts. In fact, many officers thought that hostiles other than Victorio's band were operating in the area and then gaining sanctuary either on the Mescalero Reservation or across the Mexican border. However, it mattered little to the Army or to the citizens of New Mexico who was the guilty party, for they wished only to see the depredations stopped as soon as possible.

The civilians principally blamed the Army for its failure to deter raids; however, they were particular not to place the blame on the black Cavalry. In fact, the Santa Fe *Weekly New Mexican,* on November 29, 1879, carried an editorial extolling the fighting qualities of the Ninth Cavalry. According to the paper, the black soldiers' behavior in the Victorio campaign should have ended all doubts about the effectiveness of the blacks as fighting men: "The history [of the Ninth] is a record of forced marches, endurance and bravery such as only a fine regiment in an Indian country could experience and come out of with credit. There has never been the slightest disposition to slight duty or avoid danger. Whenever called upon they have responded with remarkable energy and faithfulness." [21] The people of New Mexico were proud of the spirit and sense of duty that the Ninth exhibited. The troops in this regiment behaved as bravely as any group in the service. Still, as late as May of 1880, the people of New Mexico were speaking negatively about the federal government and its vacillating Indian policy, charging that the Territory of New Mexico had been "treated as a step child, an alien with no rightful claim upon the protection of the flag for which her people have fought and laid down their lives." [22]

At the end of March, Colonel Hatch learned from scouting reports that Victorio and his band were camped in Hembrillo Canyon, on the eastern side of the San Andres Mountains, fifty miles east of Cuchillo Negro. Hatch quickly assembled troops in this area for a final strike against the Apaches. Three companies of Apache scouts, five troops of the Ninth Cavalry, and soldiers from the Sixth Cavalry were secretly gathered for a surprise attack on the renegades. Other troops participating were those from Fort Stanton, under Captain Henry Carroll; they were supposed to block the Indian movement at the northern end of the San Andres Mountains, while Captain Curwen B. McLellan, in command of the Sixth Cavalry troop, was to move eastward at night from Aleman's Well, west of the San Andres Mountains, and reach Hembrillo Canyon by the morning of April 7. Although Hatch hoped to surprise the Victorio band, word spread that he was planning an attack.

Throughout March, the hostiles had harassed the soldiers and civilians. On March 23, 1880, a small band of Apaches attacked, killed, and mutilated a lone courier carrying messages for the Ninth Cavalry. Emboldened by this easy victory, the Apaches then attacked a party of two soldiers and three Mexicans near San José. One soldier died, but the hostiles pulled away before doing further damage.[23]

With the rest of his troops carefully deployed, Hatch decided to take his immediate command southeast from Aleman's Well to try to cut all escape routes into Mexico. Finally, Benjamin H. Grierson, colonel of the Tenth Cavalry, moving from Fort Concho and other forts in western Texas, was ordered to halt any hostile attempt to head into the very rough country southeast of the San Andres. This elaborate plan should have worked well, and in fact it would have, if it had not been for the misfortune of Captain Carroll and his troops.

En route to Hembrillo Canyon, Carroll and his troops stopped briefly at a *malpais* spring in order to refresh horses and men. Still unaware of the direction Victorio had taken, Carroll sent Lieutenant John Conline and thirty-one men of Company "A," Ninth Cavalry, to search for the Indians. Thirty-seven miles from the spring, Conline "struck Indian sign" indicating that thirty to fifty Indians were ahead. He advised Carroll by courier, then continued to follow the trail. About 5:30 p.m. he was attacked, at which time he sent additional messages to Carroll asking for help. He and his men endured a withering fire for almost two hours; then, when Victorio pulled his force back slightly, allowing a break in the firing, Conline fell back to join Carroll and the rest of the command. In this encounter Conline lost one man and two badly needed horses.[24]

Unfortunately, Carroll had no Apache scouts with him at this time. He and his men failed to realize that the water they drank that night of April 5, 1880, was gypsum water—sufficiently bad to bring extreme suffering and pain both to animals and men. By morning the next day, his command was in a pitiful state. Determined to carry out his orders, Carroll then headed for another water source that he remembered from an earlier trip into those mountains. With no medicine to quell the nausea and diarrhea, the men toiled over the tiring terrain; stopping periodically to relieve their suffering, they arrived at the place where water had been—only to find the spring dry. Their only alternative at this point was to head quickly to Hembrillo Canyon, for abundant water was known to be there. Misfortune again struck Carroll and his men, however, for they arrived at the Canyon to find not only water but also a large number of Indians. The cavalrymen and horses, weakened from suffering and the long dry march, had no opportunity to obtain water, and, even worse, had to fight for their lives.

The Indians quickly perceived that the soldiers were sick and took quick advantage of the situation. They placed themselves in such a way as to block access to the water. During the night a few brave soldiers stole forward to fill canteens with water out of the stream, but several were mortally wounded in the process. And early the next morning Carroll's command was completely surrounded by the hostiles, who were bent on annihilating them. Fortune finally smiled on the Army, however, for just at daylight Captain McLellan and elements of the Sixth Cavalry arrived in the area, heard shots, and sent Lieutenants Gatewood and Timothy Touey to investigate. Seeing the difficulties their comrades were in, these officers hurried back, brought the rest of McLellan's men up, and a hard battle ensued. Gatewood's scouts flanked the hostiles, forcing them to head for safety, while Touey's men cleared them from ledges above the spring.

Hatch, in a later report, noted that the Indians were as well armed as his troops were, "and had thrown up with much labor stone rifle pits, where there were not natural defenses." He continued, "Victorio with his band and nearly every fighting man of the Mescaleros, and some Comanches, were in the fight. Carroll's command was badly used up being nearly three days without water. Twenty-five horses and mules killed, and most of the officers' private horses." Carroll was badly wounded, and seven of his men were so severely wounded that they later died.[25]

Yet Captain McLellan praised his men for their behavior in this fight, insisting that his "detachments of the Sixth Cavalry, and the San Carlos Indian scouts acted most gallantly during the engagement." In particular, McLellan praised Lieutenants Touey, Gatewood, and Cruse for their bravery under fire. Afterward, the captain returned to Arizona without loss of a single man or animal.[26] At the end of this engagement the hostiles retreated into rough country. Following them would have been so difficult that the officers chose to rest their men before resuming the chase. These commanders insisted that "Victoria [sic] was undoubtedly present and from the number of Indians there is not a question the Mescaleros were in the fight. The Indians broke last night thoroughly whipped."[27]

Although Hatch was probably conservative in his report, he still seemed optimistic about the battle, despite the fact that his men were not in a position to bring the hostiles to surrender. The Indians did not have the firepower to fight, and the Army, having marched so far, was in no shape to continue the battle.

During the actual fight Colonel Hatch had been leading his men toward the mountains. He had no indication that a fight was taking place. He later learned of it when two couriers caught up with his troops just before they entered the ranges. Fearing that the troopers under attack might be massacred, he headed north at full speed. Unknowingly, at this juncture he missed an opportunity to entrap the hostiles and end the fight. Victorio, with many women, children, and old people, had headed south along the same trail that Hatch had followed north. The Indians saw the soldiers first and took to the earth. Years later, Nana, who had been a chief with Victorio, remembered that the entire party had had a bad fifteen minutes while the soldiers passed within shouting distance. Scouts later confirmed that the troops had indeed passed right by the Indians. After this close call, the hostiles split into three groups. One headed for the Mescalero Reservation, another into the Sacramento Mountains to the East, and the third, with Victorio along, headed south for fifteen miles and then virtually disappeared.

Actually, many of the hostiles waited until the troops left the area, then very skillfully doubled back to Aleman's Well, broke the padlocks on the water troughs, and rested for a short while. The military mistakenly assumed that the hostiles had fled into Mexico; this assumption was based on guess and past experience, not on hard evidence, for range cattle obliterated the hostiles' trail the next day.

In actuality, Victorio had returned to his old haunts in the Black Range. All the Army did know for certain at this point was that some of the renegades involved in this fight had departed eastward toward the Mescalero Reservation at Tularosa; to the soldiers this proved the Indians' complicity in and culpability for what was taking place in New Mexico.

Also apparent to Hatch at the end of March 1880 was that his campaign to date had not ended the Indian attacks. Despite the aid of Texas Rangers and Mexican militiamen, both of which groups were in the field pursuing the hostiles, the raids continued. The Ojo Caliente Apaches still had not been brought to bay. And the citizens of New Mexico, daily more critical of the Army and its efforts, as well as more suspicious than ever of Indians, even those living on the reservations, were complaining to Washington. Some even argued that a sure way to end the problem was to remove the Mescalero Apaches from the Tularosa Reservation; some suggested that these Apaches should be moved to the Indian Territory, others, that they should be sent to Florida.

Many of the officers stationed in New Mexico, along with some at command centers in the East, agreed with the civilians. No soldiers went so far as to urge removal, but many did suggest that the Indians on the reservations should be dismounted and disarmed; such a step, said these officers, would deprive Victorio and the Ojo Caliente Apaches of both recruits and supplies. Indeed, by the end of March 1880, drastic steps seemed in the offing, for the depridations committed by Victorio and his followers were considered intolerable by everyone.

6
ARMY
ATTEMPTS AT SOLUTION

Because some Mescaleros at Tularosa doubtless were helping Victorio and his people, local Army officers became more and more insistent that measures be taken to stop these Indians from joining the hostiles. Even the agent at the reservation, S. A. Russell, realized that decisive action was necessary if the Victorio band was to be captured; Russell generally agreed that some Mescalero warriors were fighting with Victorio's band, and that occasionally some of Victorio's warriors entered the reservation to see their kin held there, or else to seek supplies and volunteers. However, Russell believed that it might be a mistake to dismount these Indians, for "they will not willingly consent to it, and if accomplished by force, the Indians will afterwards retaliate upon the people in this country." [1]

During the early months of 1880, the raids continued, however, and the people of New Mexico became more outspoken. Thereupon Colonel Benjamin F. Grierson and the Tenth Cavalry, with units from Fort Concho and Fort Davis, Texas, entered New Mexico to help disarm the Mescaleros. Also, during these months, the Mexican government launched a drive to bring a final end to the Apache raids. Still, on both sides of the border very little was immediately accomplished, other than constant pursuit of the hostiles.

Colonel Grierson with 280 men of the Tenth Cavalry and fifteen men of the Twenty-fifth Infantry assigned as train guards were still in the area, and commanders asked the Department of the Army to allow the troops from Fort Concho to remain near the Mescalero Reservation in the event that trouble arose. While debate raged over whether to place all Mescaleros at Tularosa, attacks continued in southern New Mexico. W. G. Ritch, then Acting Governor of New Mexico, learned from a rancher near Socorro County that the Indians had attacked a number of civilians on March 27, 1880. According to this report the hostiles had "killed a son of Luis Lafaya of La Jolla and a herder besides two other men." Evidently the renegades indeed were wreaking havoc on the ranchers in the area.[2]

Grierson and men from Fort Concho, Texas, arrived on April 12, 1880, at the Mescalero Reservation. They were convinced that many of the Indians there had been riding with Victorio. Hatch, approaching the reservation from the West and following the largest trail from the site of a battle of April 10, also arrived at Tularosa that same day. Grierson placed his men at Hatch's disposal, and together they planned the disarming and dismounting of all Indians on the reservation. Significantly, some of the renegade Mescaleros came to the reservation voluntarily; reportedly, others would arrive the following day.

On April 16, 1880, after about 320 Mescaleros had arrived peacefully at the reservation headquarters, Hatch began to disarm the men. However, all did not go well, for the Colonel later reported that about sixty-five warriors tried to make a break for freedom on foot, and ten or more were killed. Nevertheless, thirty escaped, and troops and scouts went in hot pursuit. Many of the Mescaleros fleeing probably feared that, if caught at Tularosa, they eventually would be tried and hanged.[3] Colonel Hatch reported at the end of this search that his men had confiscated 200 ponies and mules suitable for pack-train use; in actuality, nearly 400 were taken. As the Army had no other use for the animals, the officers gave the captured stock to teamsters in Arizona and New Mexico. Also on April 16 Lieutenant Gatewood and his men intercepted a party of Mescaleros, who were allegedly running off stock. A fight ensued, and two of the Indians were killed. Agent Russell later complained that these Indians were only trying to round up stock that had escaped from the reservation, and that they had not been involved in any attack on persons or property. By the end of April, Hatch had pulled most of his troops from the Mescalero Reservation—the disarming of the Indians there had been completed—and had resumed chasing the remnants of Victorio's band. A small armed guard was left at the reservation to squelch any ensuing uprising over the disarming and dismounting.

Afterward, Colonel Grierson was allowed to take some of the confiscated animals with him and march east looking for hostiles. He scouted southeastern New Mexico, including the Sacramento and Guadalupe Mountains. During this march Grierson reported that, in his brief fights with Apaches, "two Indian Chiefs [were] killed and buried, three others shot, and from best evidence obtainable, believed to be dead; five squaws, two children, and about 50 herd of stock captured; camps destroyed and one captive Mexican boy recovered from Indians." [4] Despite such success, raiding continued. In one of these the Apaches were said to have killed eight more citizens, including women and children.

Grierson would return to his headquarters by May 8, after marching approximately 1500 miles. Major Morrow's command, still tracking hostiles, caught up with part of Victorio's band in Dog Canyon and a fierce firefight followed. Actually, the forty braves involved had been among those who had fled the reservation a few days earlier rather than be disarmed. Three of the Indians were killed and twenty-five animals were captured, yet the hostiles broke away and headed for the safety of the Guadalupe Mountains. Gatewood and his scouts were given a one-day rest—they had just marched and ridden eighty-five miles in thirty-six hours—and then were sent to track the fast-fleeing hostile forces.

Obviously, the disarming of the Indians at Tularosa reduced Victorio's ability to acquire more supplies, for neither men, guns, nor horses could be sent from the reservation to the hard-pressed hostiles.

Still all was not completely well, for Agent Russell complained to Army headquarters that Hatch was holding more than 300 Indians at Tularosa virtually as prisoners of war—and that these Indians had caused absolutely no problems. Hatch's dilemma was deciding which of the Indians had helped the renegades and which had not; moreover, Agent Russell refused to recognize or to admit the difficulty the Army had in ascertaining just who had committed the outrages. As always in war, the innocent suffered along with the guilty.

Meanwhile, during the first week in May, Hatch sent Major Morrow in pursuit of Mescaleros across the Rio Grande in the Black Range and the San Mateo Mountains. He asked Grierson to support these troops. Finally, Hatch decided to take the troops immediately under his command and go through the San Andres and Soledad Mountains searching for Victorio's trail. After five days scouring the area, however, he found no sign of the hostiles.[5]

During the last few days of April and the early days of May, Victorio seemed to have vanished. Every scouting report indicated that the hostiles were not to be found. Then reports arrived that Victorio had begun raiding again; thirteen Mexican sheepherders were slain and thousands of sheep were left untended in the Black and Mogollon ranges. The bodies, it was said had been "horribly mutilated." [6] Next, early in May, came speculation that the Indians were heading toward San Carlos. This proved correct. Forty of the hostiles were making a sweep in that direction. In this move toward San Carlos, the hostiles attacked Cooney's Camp, a mining operation on Mineral Creek in the Mogollons, and after an all-day fight Jim Cooney and two others were killed, while several others were wounded and many horses were stolen. It was reported that twenty-four Indians were killed, but this mattered little to the infuriated citizens of southern New Mexico. Captain Dan Madden of the Sixth Cavalry led Silver City "volunteers" after the Indians; one of these volunteers sent part of his diary of the expedition to the *Silver City Herald*. Marching seventy-two miles in the first twenty-four hours, the volunteers could not locate the hostiles. On the second day they found Cooney's body and two others, all

Silver City, N.M., *c.* 1890. The citizens of Silver City banded together to pursue Victorio. *Western New Mexico University Library.*

mutilated. Marching from sunrise until eleven or twelve each night, the men quickly exhausted themselves and their mounts.

Hatch did not answer Madden's request for help during this campaign, however. In fact, he was irate at the volunteers for going into the mountains. People living near Silver City heard of Hatch's displeasure and commented to the newspaper that if the Colonel "would move his command closer to them, they would try and protect him." After twelve days on the hostiles' trail, the volunteers returned to Silver City.[7] One newspaper offered some poetry poking fun at Hatch; it parodied a children's verse: "Hitchity Hatchity here I come, old

Vic's after me, but you must keep mum." [8] The editor of the Cimarron newspaper realized, however, that the military—especially Major Morrow—had not done too badly and that they had fought hard, received nothing but curses, and did not deserve such harsh criticism. [9]

On May 10, 1880, citizens living in western New Mexico near Silver City complained to President Rutherford B. Hayes about their danger. They wrote that "hostile Apaches under Victoria [sic] have been . . . reinforced from the Apache reservation. . . ." These irate citizens loudly claimed that the Indians were becoming more aggressive and merciless in their raids, and reported that fifteen of their friends had been slain and hundreds of sheep had been scattered over the area. [10]

Actually, it appeared that Victorio's band at times might even have attacked peaceful Indians living at the San Carlos Reservation. In the process of this battle Victorio's band killed a Mr. Killdegoing and his entire family, a total of twelve people. [11] Fourteen hard-riding, well-armed Apaches, probably led by Washington, who was said to be Victorio's son, raided in the area around San Carlos. [12] These hostiles may have been trying to direct members of their families away from the reservation. In the process this group skirmished with followers of Juh and Geronimo, then rejoined Victorio's main band twenty miles south of Hillsboro. [13]

Responding to the pressure of the consistent Indian attacks, the Army remained doggedly on the hostiles' trail. Finally, on May 17, 1880, Major Morrow's command, by then completely exhausted, stopped and rested on the Fresco River. H. K. Parker, a trusted leader of scouts and a crusty Indian fighter, asked Morrow for permission to continue the chase, and Morrow agreed. The army commander helped Parker outfit eight pack animals and gave him four days' rations. The mules were so weak that they collapsed after going a short distance, but Parker and his command staggered on until, on the fourth day, they came upon Colonel Hatch and his command, who were resting at Ojo Caliente. Resupplied—and encouraged by Hatch's orders to kill Indians—Parker took three more days' rations and resumed the chase.

Obviously, Hatch told Parker that the Apaches were heading east, but because the Army horses had collapsed the larger party could not then continue the chase. Hatch also knew that "the Indians are in the same condition, their trail being covered with dead horses." [14] Parker continued his pursuit, and on the second day his scouts found "sign" that the enemy had passed the Palomas River. On May 23, toward the end of the day, scouts reported they had finally found the elusive Apaches and that they were encamped on the river near the canyon headwaters of the Palomas.

Carefully, Parker divided his men and prepared an ambush. Parker told one group of men not to fire until daylight; the others would begin firing as soon as the hostiles started to flee. One sergeant was ordered to take thirty men to positions above the Indians, while Parker and eleven sharpshooters would approach from the unprotected side of the camp. At dawn the fight began, surprising the Apaches sufficiently to drive them farther back into the canyon, where they fortified their position. Victorio was with this group, and he steadfastly refused to surrender. Problems persistently plagued Parker, for at this time he had too few men to finish off the Indians. Therefore, while he tried to keep them pinned in the canyon, he sent a courier to Hatch for reinforcements.

The courier arrived safely at Hatch's previous camp, only to find that the commander had gone to Fort Craig, on the Rio Grande. When Hatch received the courier's report he telegraphed the War Department that his troops finally had struck the Indians. Hatch evidently waited for some word of the outcome of the battle. The fight began at daybreak, and shortly thereafter the hostiles realized they were in a trap and tried to hide themselves behind rocks. Intense Army firing killed several of them. The fight continued until darkness. Victorio was wounded in the leg, but he still refused to cease fighting and surrender.

With darkness descending and their food, ammunition, and water depleted, Parker and his men retreated five miles, looking for water. The weary troops camped there two nights and one day before giving up and returning to Ojo Caliente. Once the troops left, the Apaches vanished into the mountains. Hatch still had not responded. No one could guess why the commander had not sent troops, for it was learned later that the courier definitely had arrived at Hatch's camp. By this time the citizens of New Mexico and the press throughout the country were becoming exceedingly critical of the Army and its commander in New Mexico.

More news of continuing depredations came to the War Department and the press. It seemed to the newspapers that all of New Mexico and part of Arizona was a theater of war, with Indians sacking all settlements in the area. The Army denied many of the reported raids and stated that, at times, there were gross exaggerations and inconsistencies in the reports. Rumors were causing more trouble than Indians, according to some Army officials. Hatch took all these reports seriously and sent men to check stories whenever he was officially notified of them. He insisted:

> At all events all the troops at my command except those in southern Colorado which cannot now be removed, are in the field against these very Indians and their number is certainly adequate to the work of running down the Indians—it is a mere question of hunting them down as they do not keep together nor stand for a fight. Their old men, women and children are at San Carlos Agency in Arizona being fed and comfortably cared for by the government whilst the active warriors are in the field raiding with the knowledge, from past experience, that if they are too hard pressed they can go into the San Carlos Indian Agency in Arizona where they will be safe.[15]

During the last week of April and the early days of May, the newspapers continued to carry stories of Indian atrocities. According to one report, "The hardy pioneer, the loving wife and helpless child, are alike as stricken down by the fiendish Indian." Again and again the papers remarked that the military apparently was powerless to protect the citizens; "the wily Apache plays with the troops in the field, as though they were men of straw; here today, 50 miles away tomorrow, they murder as they go, and laugh at any effort of the troops to punish them." One editor stated, "It will take 5,000 troops to conquer a peace;

where are they to come from?'' According to these reports, the problem was serious—perhaps more so than the Army really cared to admit.[16]

Actually, once again many of the attacks credited to Victorio may not have been committed by Indians. In one instance two miners were found dead in southern New Mexico, and as usual the Indians were blamed. Later it was ascertained that the two men had killed each other in a brawl over a mining claim.[17] Still, it mattered little to the residents of New Mexico who committed the depredations, for they now began to have a rather low opinion of Colonel Hatch. "Something must be done; flesh and blood cannot long endure what we as a people are now enduring. If we have an imbecile in command of our forces, let us try by all honorable means to have him removed." When the newspaper editorials were not blaming Hatch they were attacking the Ninth and Tenth Cavalry. As one editor wrote, the area was left "to depend upon two parts of regiments of colored troops, Buffalo soldiers as old Victorio calls them, who have already shown themselves not to be equal to the occasion, and as there is no likelihood that our situation will be any better for some months to come, but really be getting worse and worse, we must look to our own defense at least." [18]

The citizens of Silver City had asked for government help and then had organized a volunteer group to track the hostiles. Still Victorio remained free. Albert J. Fountain, a New Mexican, worked hard to organize local militia to protect the Mesilla Valley from Victorio's raids. The besieged citizens cooperated, for most of them believed that extermination was the only way to deal with hostile Indians.[19] Still, efforts like those of Fountain made the Army's task no easier. Complicating matters was the fact that Governor Lew Wallace periodically left the territory; at this time he was in Washington asking for help in ending the conflict in New Mexico. While he was gone during the first half of 1880, the Indian raids were worse than ever, and people became outraged at his absence at such a critical time. Previously, in an address to the people of New Mexico, Governor Wallace had blamed Indian difficulties on the very nature of the Apaches.

While the people attacked the Governor, they also blamed the Army, especially Colonel Hatch, for failing to stop Indian attacks. Citizens of Grant County met and condemned Hatch's actions in the field. They also insisted that Hatch's reports were exaggerated, and, joining in the campaign led by the editor of *Thirty-Four,* they insisted on Hatch's removal. According to those who wanted a new commander for the area, Hatch was only trying to impress his superiors by avoiding fights and thereby avoiding losses; by so doing he was seeking promotion and other personal benefits.[20] The editor of *Thirty-Four* satirically suggested that a new periodical called "The Apache Chronicle" was being published in southwestern New Mexico. There were such stories as this: "Gratifying if true—our braves will be pleased to learn that it is reported that our esteemed friend Captain Beyer has been ordered to take the field with a fresh pack train and a large supply of ammunition. This intelligence we hope to be true, as our young warriors have wasted considerable ammunition lately, shooting cattle." The periodical humorously reported that the Army sent a note requesting 10,000 more men, so that the campaign would be wrapped up "within the present century—signed, Scratch, Dist. Commander." [21]

By the end of May 1880, however, a few realistic appraisals were being made. According to the Santa Fe *Weekly New Mexican,* Hatch had taken personal command of his men and had "taken a carbine and marched on the trail of Victoria [sic], and yet each day sees him with a smaller force and one less prepared to conquer the Indians." [22]

Hatch had not been idle during the days when these derisive complaints were being made. He reported his progress many times to the Department of the Army. The story was rather sad at times. In one report Hatch allowed that the Indians had led his men on such a wild and difficult chase that the horses had collapsed, forcing his weary men to continue on foot. That method of transport was totally unacceptable for the desert regions of the Southwest, however, for the men were soon so footsore that they were unable to continue. In order to facilitate tracking down the hostiles, the Army high command agreed to let Grierson and his five companies of cavalry, along with scouts, at Fort Stanton continue the chase.[23] Likewise, other troops were sent from the Indian Territory and even from Kansas to join the fight.

In all fairness to the Army, the complaining citizens of New Mexico overlooked the victories scored during the month of May by Hatch and his troops. Especially significant was that of Parker at Cañada Alamosa, at the head of the Palomas River, late in May. Progress was being made; moreover, the victories, coupled with the disarming and dismounting of the Mescaleros, marked the real beginning of the demise of the Victorio band. Parker had actually captured seventy-four horses, had had no manpower losses in his group, and had caused the Victorio group to divide; some of the hostiles joined more peaceful Indians on reservations. However, complete victory once again eluded the Army, and the deceptive Victorio headed south for Mexico, pillaging and plundering as he traveled.[24]

Hatch requested authority to recruit fifty more Indian scouts to help track the hostiles. On May 31 he reported that four companies—reduced to about 100 men—and Indian scouts were chasing the hostiles south toward Mexico. According to his estimate, there were about 100 warriors in the party. He was not certain whether this was Victorio's band or whether these were Indians from Mexico heading home across the border. However, he was optimistic about trapping this group, and perhaps even Victorio, before they crossed the border. Actually he was only conjecturing concerning the whereabouts of the band, for his troops did not in fact catch the hostiles until early in June.[25]

As the hostiles headed quickly for Mexico, they stopped long enough at the west end of Cook's Canyon to kill five men who happened to be in their path. On June 4, at Silver City, New Mexico, local citizens joined to write a petition to the Army asking for changes. These worried citizens insisted that Victorio had departed the reservation in April of 1879 with only some sixty warriors, but as the Army had been ineffective in stopping their raiding, younger members of other Apache tribes, had joined his ranks. These civilians even insisted that some Navajos had also joined the Apache leader, and that the hostile strength was estimated at 500 to 800 men. Moreover, according to this group, "since the war began, about 200 of the people of southern New Mexico have been killed." They charged that Colonel Hatch, commanding the District of New Mexico, had misrepresented his successes by describing victories over "Indians, which have never been achieved, and has made reports which are untruthful throughout." [26]

By June, 1880, the citizens of New Mexico were so chagrined at the performance of the Army and the United States government in dealing with the hostiles that hate editorials were being printed almost daily in regional newspapers. Economics may have played a significant part in local disenchantment with the Army, for mining and general commerce had been severely limited as a result of the raids.[27] Citizens adamantly charged:

> No other nation that ever existed on the globe and made any pretensions to civilization would have allowed its poorest down-trodden serfs to have been subjected to such a reign of devastation, murder and raping as have been and are still the people of this territory. . . . In the name of peace, in the name of an unprotected people; in the name of the surviving families of those who have paid the forfeit of their lives for attempting to develop the resources of this rich territory; in the name of the thousands who now desire to make New Mexico their homes but are deterred by these fearful tidings, we ask that a sufficient force be sent here to prevent the threatened outbreak, and keep those bloodthirsty demons within their proper bounds.[28]

No matter how heated the criticism, the soldiers remained on the trail of the hostiles. On June 5, Major Morrow and four troops of the Ninth Cavalry caught up with Victorio in Cook's Canyon, near Fort Cummings. A battle ensued in which two hostiles were killed and three wounded. A large number of horses and other livestock were also captured. One of the Indians killed in the battle was said to be Victorio's son Washington.[29] By this time local army officers were also tired of the problems with the Indians and were determined to organize the greatest manhunt in the history of the area. In fact, by this time hundreds of Mexican regulars were aiding the Army, while Texas Rangers, civilian posses, and others joined the search—all bent on punishing the hostiles for the previous raids. Major Morrow and his command, meanwhile, doggedly followed the hostiles to within seven miles of the border, near Fort Cummings, and the Indians, numbering about 100, headed for Laguna Palomas, Chihuahua. Despite the criticism of Hatch, he kept men pursuing the renegades until they fled south of the border.[30]

After entering Mexico the hostiles attacked property of the Governor of Chihuahua at San Lorenzo. There they killed more than 100 horses. West of San Carlos other horses were killed, and in the process a number of Mexicans reportedly became victims of the Apache wrath. In response to the attacks in Chihuahua, the Governor of that state took the field at the head of troops. With 200 men, among them federal soldiers and local volunteers, the Governor scoured the area looking for the renegades. State officials in Chihuahua implored all citizens to be courageous and defend "against the fierce barbarian, their honor, their families, their homes, their lives, and their country." [31]

By 1878, when Don Joaquín Terrazas, a man who had dedicated his life to fighting Indians, was asked to organize the frontier, Mexico had experienced all it would tolerate from Apache raiders. Terrazas was born in Chihuahua in 1829, and he evidently grew to manhood with an intense dislike of Indians—especially the Apaches that plagued the border regions of his native state. A thin man with small piercing eyes and a dark mustache, he was a tenacious and honorable soldier. In 1850, he dedicated himself to fighting these Indians. Politically, Joaquín Terrazas was a liberal who supported the Mexican federal system, just as Luis Terrazas was. During the war of the Reform in 1857 he had fought for the liberal forces. He remained loyal to the federal government and eventually fought the conservatives who suggested the Plan de la Noria and the Plan of Tuxtepec, both of which reflected Porfirio Díaz's desires concerning the Mexican presidency. Terrazas had gained considerable frontier experience as a member of units guarding shipments and riding escort for travelers between Paso del Norte (present-day Juárez) and Chihuahua City. According to José C. Chávez, Terrazas was for Chihuahua *"el denodado Paladin,"* whose decisive actions would result in Victorio's death at Tres Castillos.[32]

On May 27, 1880, soon after General Don Luis Terrazas had become Governor of Chihuahua, he announced to his constituents that Victorio once again had entered Mexico and was then camped at Guzman and Santa María Lakes. The Governor asked for support to put troops in the field against "this fierce and irreconcilable enemy of humanity. . . ." [33] He reported that Colonel Adolfo J. Valle was in the field, but that more troops were needed. Actually, there was some disagreement between Valle, representing federal troops, and Terrazas. A patriotic promulgation was issued, one designed to get citizen support for the campaign. The Governor turned again to Don Joaquín Terrazas to lead these forces. A meeting between Terrazas and Colonel Valle took place August 23, 1880. However, the two Mexican leaders could not agree on what to do. Valle said that every time he chased the Apaches they headed for the United States and safety. Terrazas thereupon proposed that part of the federal troops and fifty horses that had been in a previous fight at Carrizal be turned over to him for use in his pursuit. Valle insisted his men and animals were too exhausted. They must rest. The meeting ended without agreement. The next day Governor Terrazas talked with Don Simón Amaya, political chieftain of the Canton of Guerrero; Amaya promised full support to Terrazas and troops were quickly organized. The Governor told Joaquín Terrazas of his plan to concentrate troops in the north and Terrazas agreed with the strategy.

The state force, with Joaquín Terrazas in command, departed Chihuahua City on September 25, 1880, heading for San Andres. The soldiers passed through a number of villages and in Corralitos, Terrazas met and joined up with Captain Gordo and his command of 119 men. On September 29, 1880, more men joined at Carrizal, bringing the total to 350 volunteers. Then, careful not to force Victorio's band to flee, this army marched toward the reported location of Victorio's camp.

With Mexicans and Americans on the alert on both sides of the border, the Apaches still managed to disappear. Avoiding Chihuahua City, the hostiles went thirty miles north and then camped some fifty miles away. The United States Army had a temporary breather, but Hatch predicted that Mexicans would soon force the hostiles to recross the border—probably into Texas below El Paso. Stationed at Fort Davis, in the Davis Mountains, Colonel Grierson was apprised during July of the difficulties in New Mexico and told that very likely the Indians would arrive in his area shortly. Thus, just as Hatch had done, Grierson prepared to block the re-entry of the hostiles into the United States.

Hatch still believed that he needed permission to cross the border and chase the Indians into Mexico to defeat them. Such permission was difficult to obtain, however. The commander knew that the Indians were resting in the mountains in Mexico, nursing their sick and wounded, and he was certain that as soon as they recovered they would return to the United States. Only if he could get permission to harass them in Mexico before they could rest would it be possible to bring them to terms.[34]

During June and July additional problems with the Mescaleros in New Mexico stirred Indian Agent S. A. Russell to complain to the government that Colonel Hatch was guilty of cruelty in dealing with the Indians. The reason for this charge is obscure; however, Army reports of the time indicate the shortened tempers of the troops stationed near reservations. Hatch reported that as early as February, Indians had attacked Lieutenant Gatewood and his scouts. The hostiles later proved to be from the Mescalero reservation. In addition, the Apaches were reported using Winchester rifles, while the Army had guns from an earlier age. Moreover, it was said that a woman was wounded in the affair and original reports may have indicated that more than one woman was killed and that their deaths were unnecessary. Hatch insisted that only one woman had been wounded in the affair, and that she had been shot in the melee that followed after some of the Indians refused to lay down their rifles, instead breaking for the cover of the mountains. Stock recovered from this group had been stolen from Texas—in particular, from settlements along the Pecos River.

Indian attacks continued throughout March. Hatch reported that a soldier of the Ninth Cavalry on courier duty had been killed. About a month later a dead Mescalero Indian was found to have been carrying the carbine that had belonged to the soldier. These Mescaleros were also fighting with citizens at Tularosa and generally causing difficulties.[35] Mexicans living at Tularosa had fought the hostiles about one mile from town, killing three Indians and a number of horses. Still Agent Russell defended the Mescaleros. He insisted that while a few of them occasionally rode with Victorio, he had no doubt that the majority neither joined nor sympathized with the renegades.[36]

These Indians, however, may not have been totally happy with their agent, for military reports earlier had indicated that problems were developing between Russell and his charges. One Army officer wrote that Mescaleros were unhappy because the agent "has forbidden them to make *'tiswin,'* refuses them horses to go hunting off the reservation and will not give them beef to make a feast, or allow them to trade for vegetables." Furthermore, this report stated, some of the Indians thought of Russell as "an old woman, who did not know the Apaches and was afraid of them, that he could talk neither Apache nor Spanish and that the interpreter told him what he pleased. . . ."[37]

While Army officers argued with Russell there were yet more allegations hurled at Colonel Hatch, not the least of which branded him a coward. Hatch may not have had the respect and support of all the citizens of New Mexico or all the Indian commissioners, but he certainly had the wholehearted support of General John Pope, commander of the Division of the Missouri. Pope insisted to Army superiors that many of the rumors of Indian hostilities were greatly exaggerated. Even when the rumors were partially true, Pope defended his field commander. He said that Hatch could not be directly responsible for each isolated attack on sheepherders, and besides, Colonel Grierson with five companies of the Tenth Cavalry was scouting in the part of New Mexico between Fort Stanton and El Paso and the Pecos River, and he too had been unsuccessful in defeating the hostiles. In fact, none of these soldiers had been able to accomplish more than follow the Indians after a raid and hope they might catch up briefly for a battle. The hostiles could roam almost undetected in that largely unpopulated and wild section of New Mexico.

Pope particularly did not like the allegations of a Mr. Ashenfelter, who accused Hatch of failure, for he himself considered Hatch "a most energetic, gallant and efficient officer." He wrote, "I shall at once send the Inspector of this Department to make careful investigation of the statements of Mr. A. and will myself go to New Mexico, to see the authorities there and ascertain whether they concur in Mr. A's statements, which I do not at all believe." [38] In a final defense of his field commander, Pope enclosed a copy of a Joint Resolution of the council and House of Representatives of the Territory of New Mexico, which praised Hatch for his efforts.

Pope, who commanded the Division of the Missouri, under which the Department of New Mexico was headquartered during this era, decided to go to New Mexico and see for himself what was occurring. He arrived during the last week of June 1880, and visited with Hatch. Pope agreed to send reinforcements to the area, eventually bringing the command to nearly 2000 men. At least 1500 of these would be stationed in New Mexico, the rest to be near by, in Texas or perhaps in Colorado. Pope suggested that a barrier be stretched across southern New Mexico and that scouting parties be sent southward from the line. In addition, a new military post was to be constructed on the Rio Marcos (Marcos) in Colorado. This new post would be under Hatch's command. Thus Pope still confidently believed Hatch was doing the best possible job. And the two men, Pope and Hatch, believed that with the additional manpower and the change in strategy, the Apaches could be tracked and defeated.[39]

Not all Army officers agreed with Pope's assessment of Hatch, for General Eugene A. Carr had severely criticized the commander. Carr's Sixth Cavalry, based at Fort Bowie, Arizona, had helped track the hostiles during March. Carr reported that after searching for the hostiles' trail for several days, he had decided to check with Hatch to see if the Indians had gone east. Hatch had failed to respond. Moreover, Captain Dan Madden, leading a company of Sixth Cavalry and some volunteers from Silver City, believed that Hatch was not at all cooperative. According to Madden, his couriers had delivered messages to Hatch, and the Colonel had "turned his back upon them with the utmost discourtesy and disrespect." The couriers spoke with him again the next day and were met with similar treatment, if not worse. Madden wrote, "I was informed that . . . Hatch remained inactive here for three days. If this is so, he no doubt had his own good reasons for so doing but I am of the opinion that had or could his force have been pushed vigorously forward immediately on their arrival at the Frisco, the Indians would not have escaped as they did." [40] Hatch, who possibly was faced with insurmountable difficulties, apparently was unable to take the necessary moves to end the chase as soon as possible.

Meanwhile, Agent Russell at Tularosa had not given up in his attempt to get the Indians under his care released. They had been held virtually as prisoners of war since arriving at the reservation. Colonel Hatch felt that these Mescaleros had contributed to Victorio's success and must therefore be held in check while the hostiles were loose. In June 1880, Russell wrote the Commissioner of Indian Affairs that the Indians were complaining bitterly about being detained. He claimed that "a few days since, one of these Indians said to a White man with whom he was conversing 'When a white man steals a horse or kills anybody, you put him in the calaboos' [sic] dont you'—Yes, if we can catch him was the reply, 'You dont take all the white men there is in that country and put them in the calaboose' no we dont do that; then, said the Indian, why do you do that with the Indians?'' [41]

Apparently, only the Army was pleased with Hatch's efforts to halt the Apache raids. The citizens of Silver City, New Mexico, were asking Washington for Hatch's removal and for permission to deal with the hostiles as the people in the area wished. These disgusted souls even went so far as to write to the editors of several eastern papers seeking publicity of their trials and tribulations. The *Republican* of St. Louis carried a letter from these people, blasting the government. In particular, Colonel Hatch was criticized. According to one letter, Hatch "and his subordinate officers (Major Morrow in particular) keep up a masterly inactivity. The officers in command in New Mexico never go from one fort to another without an escort, as in the case of Major Morrow who had with him six companies of cavalry through Cook's Canyon on the 25th of May." "The People of New Mexico demand of the United States government either the removal of General Hatch from New Mexico or that they be permitted to deal with the Indians as they may find it necessary, even to extermination." [42]

Late in July, the United States Army commanders—particularly Grierson—learned that Colonel Adolph J. Valle, commanding Mexican troops, was campaigning against Victorio. Valle had 370 cavalry and 150 infantry, most of whom were Mexican federal troops, not volunteer state militia. [43] Furthermore, Valle claimed to have full permission from the United States government to cross the international border while in "hot pursuit of the hostiles." Grierson, continuing his patrols along the border and operating out of Fort Davis, sent out an offer of full cooperation with the Mexicans. Meanwhile, Colonel Hatch also learned of the Mexican efforts, and he telegraphed the Army command in Washington that he had been told that the Mexicans had about 400 men in the field. Again Hatch was late receiving information or acting upon it. [44]

Actually, the Mexicans were chasing the hostiles northward, and Army officers in New Mexico assumed that both parties would cross the Rio Grande soon, perhaps heading for Eagle Springs. Colonel Grierson force-marched his men to that location, hoping for a confrontation. [45]

Hatch and his command in New Mexico had known since the end of

June that Victorio's group was in Mexico. Moreover, the Army knew that the Apaches had made fierce attacks on ranches and settlements in Chihuahua. Luis Terrazas, Governor of that state, reported that the Apaches even had attacked his San Lorenzo Ranch and had slaughtered nearly 100 horses and had killed several Mexicans. After attacking this ranch, which was located thirty miles north of Chihuahua, the Apaches apparently turned south and attacked other ranches, killing herders and driving off stock. However, about July 20, 1880, nearly fifty miles below Eagle Springs at a place called Ojo del Pino, Valle and his Mexican soldiers caught up with the hostiles and fought them. In this engagement Mexican soldiers lost their lives and four Indians were killed—and the pursuit started again. Two hundred armed Mexicans followed the hostiles northward toward Fort Quitman.

Meanwhile, Grierson had positioned his troops along the Rio Grande, where he hoped to stop the northward advance of the hostiles. Colonel Valle reported to Grierson and Hatch that a small Mexican cavalry patrol had located a few hostiles near the Pine Mountains on July 26, and had killed more of the Indians. Grierson had a similar experience while leading a small six-man patrol near Fort Quitman on July 27. He learned of the presence of a large party of Indians heading north toward the Rio Grande, and determined to block their passage northward. While Grierson was replenishing his water supplies in Quitman Canyon at Tinaja de las Palmas, a courier arrived with word from Captain John C. Gilmore, at Eagle Springs, that Victorio and 150 warriors were riding up Quitman Canyon. Victorio was heading directly toward Grierson's position. Grierson had with him only six men, one of whom was his son Robert. Nevertheless, he positioned his men in ambush at the waterhole and waited for the Indians.

Stagecoaches passing during the night carried word to Fort Quitman and Eagle Springs of the approaching hostiles. Lieutenant Leighton Finley, accompanied by fifteen troopers, made a forced march to arrive at the waterhole at 4 a.m. Then, realizing that twenty-five men could not easily hold the site, Grierson sent two men back to Quitman with orders to bring all available men. Somehow, once again, the Army erred, for Grierson received only a small escort—too few to assault and defeat the larger Indian band.[46]

Grierson was not completely discouraged, but by this time the hostiles had learned of the Army's presence. Nevertheless, they approached the waterhole, and Grierson had no recourse left but to attack with what men he had. There were at least sixty hostiles, and the Army was sorely outnumbered. With no other plan to follow, Grierson sent Lieutenant Leighton Finley with a detachment of ten men to charge the Indian position, hoping to drive them away. For more than an hour the fight was carried to the Indians, but after the initial charge, Finley and his men were driven back across the river. Imminent disaster faced the troops. Fortunately, about one hour later, Captain Charles Viele with Troops "C" and "G" of the Tenth Cavalry arrived to join the hard-pressed troops. Viele's men thought Finley's men were the hostiles, and they loosed a deadly fire for a few seconds before learning of their error. At this opportunity, the Apaches charged. Soon Captain Nicholas Nolan and Troop "A" of the Tenth Cavalry arrived from Fort Quitman and entered the fight. The arrival of yet more soldiers caused the hostiles immediately to break off the engagement and head south toward the Rio Grande.

Lieutenant Henry O. Flipper, the only black officer in the United States Army at this time, participated in the battle of Quitman Canyon, and thereby had the opportunity to show his devotion to duty. Flipper's troop of the Tenth Cavalry had been sent first to Fort Davis, in the spring of 1880, and later to Fort Quitman. In one instance, when Apaches surprised troops on the Rio Grande and successfully ran off most of the horse herd, Flipper had ridden to Eagle Springs with a message for Grierson. He dashed ninety-eight miles through the Apache-infested desert, arrived at his destination, rested briefly, mounted a fresh horse, and rode the return trip to his unit. Moreover, with obvious disregard for personal danger, Flipper performed well under pressure, for it was just after Grierson came under attack in the canyon that Flipper made another fast ride. He led reinforcements to

Quitman Canyon along with Captain Nolan. During his service as a lieutenant in the Tenth Cavalry, Flipper participated in several battles and short campaigns. Unfortunately, he later was forced to resign from the Army; he was charged with culpability for alleged irregularities in accounting for post funds. He was probably innocent of charges, but he had little opportunity to exonerate himself.

One soldier died in the fight at Quitman Canyon and four were wounded, while Victorio suffered about seven killed. During this nearly three-hour battle both sides suffered casualties, but neither achieved a decisive victory.[47]

Grierson again misjudged the hostiles, for by August 4, 1880, the Indians had slipped through the network of troops, skirmished briefly with other soldiers scouting the area, and pushed north once again. Victorio actually retreated toward the Guadalupe Mountains, and on the afternoon of August 4, crossed the El Paso Road ten miles east of Van Horn's Wells. Grierson was about four hours behind the hostiles.[48] Meanwhile, the Mexican troops had decided to stop their pursuit in the United States and return to Chihuahua. They were seen passing near Fort Quitman, and they verified that fact that Victorio had indeed passed north of Quitman with perhaps as many as 150 in his band.[49]

Victorio and his followers evidently camped temporarily opposite Del Alamo, in the mountains in New Mexico near the Rio Grande. Colonel Valle was advised of the hostiles' whereabouts, but situated as he was, opposite Ojo Caliente, he was not in place to bring a decisive force to bear on the enemy. Moreover, the Rio Grande had risen, to a height almost impossible to cross.[50]

The hostiles continued northward from the border. Grierson knew the direction they were going in, and he stayed on the other side of the mountains, out of sight, following a parallel route. From his camp at Van Horn, Texas, Grierson began his march at three in the morning and continuing until the following midnight. He arrived at Rattlesnake Springs after having marched sixty-five miles in less than twenty-four hours. He arrived sufficiently ahead of the Indians to prepare an elaborate ambush; the hostiles were unaware of the Army's presence. Early on the morning of August 6, 1880, Captain Charles D. Viele divided his companies and positioned the men above the waterholes on either side of the ravine. Though tired and weary, their senses dulled by the long march, the soldiers waited patiently. When the Apaches approached the area, Captain Viele and his command, laying in ambush, began firing. At the first volley, loosed before the hostiles were in range, the Indians were thrown into the wildest disorder and sought safety in every direction. But they soon estimated the strength of the troops and began to work their way back toward the water.

As the Indians straggled toward the waterholes, still beyond the range of the Army rifles, the soldiers loosed the first of eight heavy volleys. The range was yet too great and the Indians simply scampered for cover in the near-by mountains. As the battle increased in intensity, the hostiles again tried to capture the waterhole, whereupon men under command of Lieutenant Thaddeus W. Jones concentrated their fire and drove the Indians from the battle site. The Apaches again took cover in the boulders surrounding the waterholes. Well-concealed for the next two hours, the Indians had not the strength to charge again; the soldiers too did not have the stamina to push an attack.

The Indians were soon at a strong disadvantage, however, for about four in the afternoon a supply train escorted by Captain J. C. Gilmore with men of the Twenty-fourth Infantry appeared about eight miles to the southeast, heading for the waterholes. The Indians learned of the approaching wagons and sent a party of warriors to intercept the supplies. Soldiers riding with the train did not know of the fight; they were heading directly for water. Most of the military escort was riding in the wagons, completely out of sight. The sudden appearance of soldiers pouring out of the wagons surprised the attacking hostiles. One Indian was immediately killed and several others were wounded. Other Apaches coming from the opposite side of the canyon were surprised and driven off.

Unable to overrun the troops' position, and tired and thirsty from the long chase, the hostiles headed off toward the Carrizo Mountains, northesast of Fort Quitman. Several Indians in the Victorio group had been killed. At least four had been seen falling from their horses in the earlier fray. Still, no accurate count of dead hostiles could be made because the renegades took their dead and wounded with them. Fortunately for the Army, no troops had been killed in the battle. Knowing that the Indians still badly needed water to continue their flight, Grierson sent troopers to all the waterholes in the near-by mountains. Captain L. H. Carpenter and three companies were sent to Sulphur Springs, Captain N. Nolan was detailed to Carrizos, and Captain Thomas C. Lebo was sent to scout the country between Rattlesnake Springs and Sulphur Springs. Lebo and his men were the only troops to strike Victorio. On August 9, they fell on the unsuspecting Indian camp, capturing equipment, twenty-five head of cattle, and other supplies the Indians badly needed. The Apaches scattered and sought sanctuary across the Rio Grande in Mexico. Grierson reported that the hostiles were obviously "demoralized" and had lost perhaps 100 animals. All told, Grierson's men from "K" Company, Tenth Cavalry, had given a good account of themselves in the battle.[51]

By the end of August 1880, it was obvious to parties on both sides of the border that Victorio was suffering from the constant chasing. Moreover, the disarming and dismounting of the Mescaleros at the Tularosa reservation had effectively dried up much of his supply source. Still, although most of Victorio's band crossed into Mexico during the last few days of August, some scattered warriors continued to attack citizens and settlements in New Mexico. However, with the pressure mounting it was only a matter of time until the Apache chief would come to his final battleground.

7
THE FINAL CAMPAIGN

With most of Victorio's band in Mexico, the United States Cavalry made plans to form a wall against the possible return of the hostiles, and they began to scout the area, fighting scattered bands of Apache warriors still conducting isolated raids north of the border, in New Mexico. Although Victorio's band was probably sixty miles into Mexico, conditions remained so unsafe that travel from El Paso to Silver City without military escort was impossible—the danger was too extreme. Whether Victorio's band intermittently crossed back into the United States to commit some of these acts of depredation was not known. Which particular band was guilty of any given raid mattered little to the Army, for it was responsible for trying to maintain an over-all semblance of peace and safety along the frontier.

In one incident, a serious one, unidentified hostiles attacked an overland stagecoach near Fort Quitman on August 9, 1880, and retired Brevet Major General James J. Byrne, now an employee of the Texas and Pacific Railroad, was mortally wounded by the Indians' first volley. The stage driver quickly turned his coach around and, with the General's body hanging out the door, drove his mules wildly for five miles to an adobe depot, where he found safety from the pursuing hostiles. Texas Ranger James G. Gillett later said he examined the coach and found it shot full of holes. Driver Walde, anxious for revenge, joined Lieutenant George W. Baylor's Texas Rangers in pursuing the renegades who had committed this raid. After attacking the stage, this group of hostiles crossed into Mexico, raided Jesus Cota's Ranch, shot a herder, killed a number of cattle, drove off 140 head of stock, and headed in the direction of the Candelaría Mountains of Chihuahua. When about forty head of stock mired in mud crossing the river, the starving Indians cut hunks of meat out of them and left them standing there to die.

Then, early in August, a band of Indians attacked another stage-coach, this one sixteen miles west of Fort Cummings, and a number of casualties resulted. Alexander Le Beau, the driver, and two passengers, Emery S. Madden, the son of Dan Madden of the Sixth Cavalry, and Isaac Robrs died in the attack. Pursuing soldiers caught up with the attackers, fought briefly, and lost two scouts and one soldier; Indian losses were not verified.[1]

Colonel Benjamin Grierson argued that the Apache hostiles who had fled into Mexico had been hurt badly in their recent skirmishes in New Mexico, Texas, and Chihuahua. He reported on August 25, 1880:

> Further investigation shows that Victoria [sic] and his marauders were very severely punished during their short stay in Texas. The hurried manner in which they cut and tore the flesh from dead animals found in their camp on the trail indicated the food they were compelled to subsist on after their supplies were captured by the troops in the Sierra Diablo.[2]

On August 2, 1880, Lieutenant Baylor had gathered fourteen Texas Rangers and departed for a two-week campaign. He had been notified by Colonel Grierson, who had received word from the Mexican government, that Victorio had moved into Texas in June. Grierson telegraphed Baylor that he and his men should scout the area near Eagle Springs for the Indians' trail. The next day, after riding many hard miles, the Rangers arrived at the site where the United States Army had previously fought the hostiles. Several dead cavalry horses, bullet marks on the near-by rocks, and spots of blood were all that showed that the Indians had been there. Baylor also noticed the fortified positions from which Grierson and seven men had held the hostiles from the waterhole. Then, with no hard plan and no specific destination, the Rangers traveled east toward Van Horn.

En route to this town the Rangers crossed the trail where the Indians had waylaid the stage, killed the driver and his passengers, and mutilated the dead by stuffing letters taken from mail sacks into their wounds. The Rangers were unhappy, for they seemed always to arrive after the battles had ended. In the next few days these Texans again found the hostiles' trail, and as they followed it they learned why the military telegraph was at the moment inoperative. Victorio had torn down the lines and, to delay repair, had directed his men to haul the poles three or four miles away from their original places. When the Rangers arrived at Van Horn, somewhat tired and disappointed at finding no Apaches to fight, they were surprised to learn that Grierson was not there. Baylor thereupon decided to follow Grierson, hoping to find him in time to join in any ensuing fight. Baylor did catch up with Captain Livermore and a supply train, and, since this train was armed with a Gatling gun, the Rangers hoped that the Indians would be fools enough to attack them in open country. No hostiles were seen, however, and the combined force soon overtook Colonel Grierson and his column at Rattlesnake Springs, about twenty miles from Zimpleman Salt Lake. It soon became apparent to soldiers and Rangers that the renegades once again were fleeing toward Mexico.[3]

Grierson immediately organized search parties and followed southward. Again the soldiers were unable to catch the fast-riding Apache warriors, and again civilians mounted widespread criticism of the Army and its seemingly constant inability to catch the raiders. As the summer of 1880 dragged slowly into August, the territorial press in New Mexico and Arizona became more abusive toward the Army than ever before. These civilians seem to have been unaware that, although negotiations were underway to allow troops to cross into Mexico when in active pursuit of hostiles, the Army could not legally follow Victorio southward. And the Texas Rangers, who numbered less than twenty, were too few to attack the hostiles deep in Mexico despite their special disregard of international niceties.

Also during the summer of 1880, a reappraisal of government policies at San Carlos, as well as a look at the effectiveness of the Army in dealing with Indian difficulties, took place. Government officials were chagrined at the damage caused to the Army's reputation in the preceding few months; in fact, the Indians' success seemed to encourage hostiles living on reservations to join raids both in Mexico and in the United States. The Indian agent at San Carlos, J. C. Tiffany, in July 1880 explained the Army's difficulty: he reported that "our troops so heavily burdened and moving en masse could effect but little against Indians living as they do, moving quickly by night and always on the alert." This agent believed that Victorio would not consent to return to the reservation without a fight because "he would be in danger of his life from the San Carlos Indians, he having killed a number of their tribe," including, on his last raid at Ash Creek, one of their most popular chiefs. "For this they had vowed to shoot him upon the first opportunity, anywhere." [4]

On August 26, 1880, Colonel Grierson reported that he was at Fort Quitman, scouting in that general area. He had found the bodies of several Indians as well as a number of fresh graves along the trail, indicating that the Indians had suffered severely from their recent and bloody skirmishes with the Army. He noted that the hostiles apparently had gone into the Candalaría Mountains in Mexico. What he learned from his scouts convinced him that the renegades were badly crippled and demoralized. In fact, he concluded that their stock had "played out," which was evidence of the hardship they had suffered. The American commander at San Antonio, General E. O. C. Ord, forwarded part of Grierson's report to Washington, adding to it that he had learned that the Mexican troops evidently had no inclination to attack the Indians, or, for that matter, even to get in the path of the hostiles. He also had ascertained from other sources that the Indians had lost at least thirty, killed in the battles during July and August— and perhaps more. In addition, a large number of warriors had been seriously wounded during the preceding months. Ord wrote that the Indians were thought to be about 150 miles west of Fort Quitman.[5]

By the end of August the United States' side of the border was quiet, for the Indians were to the south, raiding in Mexico. General Pope, commander of the division, declared that he had sufficient troops along the border to stop the hostiles, should they try to return to the United States. At this point the Army commanders thought they had finally obtained permission to cross the border if in hot pursuit of the enemy; yet even this permission was suspect. There was some doubt that a dispatch from Colonel Adolfo Valle allowing United States troops to cross the border had been interpreted correctly. Therefore, until this issue could be cleared up, American soldiers were to remain north of the border.

Reports continued to arrive at Army headquarters in New Mexico of sporadic Indian attacks on soldiers and private citizens; allegedly, these were committed by Victorio's band. For example, twenty miles south of Fort Cummings early in September hostiles surprised part of a company of cavalry, killing several soldiers and two scouts. The perpetrators of this attack had a fifteen-mile head start on the pursuing column, and consequently the cavalry was unable to overtake them, partly because of a water and supply shortage. Isolated incidents of this kind continued to occur with frequency. Yet Victorio's band probably was not guilty of all the reported attacks; Indians from the nearby Mescalero reservation might have perpetrated these raids. Local military commanders insisted that the only way to end this sporadic violence was to bring Victorio to terms, and to accomplish this they felt it would be necessary to have permission to cross into Mexico to pursue the hostiles.[6]

There was a precedent for United States entry into Mexico in pursuit of Indians across the border. As early as 1877, General William Tecumseh Sherman received presidential instructions to this effect. At that time there had been so many raids into the United States, and so many Indians had crossed into Mexico for safety, that the President had decided it was time to act. At that time General Sherman had told

General E. O. C. Ord, commanding the Department of Texas, to inform Mexican authorities that the United States no longer would tolerate the raiders' seeking sanctuary in Mexico. If the Mexicans would not cooperate in ending this plague, then American troops would cross the border. Ord was told his soldiers were at liberty to cross the border when in hot pursuit, or when following a fresh trail. Moreover, these troops were to punish the Indians and recapture any stolen property that had been taken to Mexico.[7]

Although the Mexicans definitely could have used this help by American troops, most of them strongly opposed it; in August 1880, political conditions were very unstable in Mexico. The American consul in Chihuahua City described the situation to his superiors in Washington: "The administration of justice, the basis of the happiness and welfare of all nations, is generally very bad in the [Mexican] states; but worse almost depraved in the Federal District." [8] With local conditions in a state of turmoil, Mexican officials adamantly refused to give the Americans official permission to bring large numbers of troops into the region. Colonel Baylor and his Texas Rangers had been allowed, unofficially, to cross the line because there were only fourteen of them—hardly a threat to Mexican national security.

As late as September 1880, American representatives in Mexico City were seeking permission for soldiers to cross the border from President Porfirio Díaz, but the Mexican leader refused the request. Mexican newspapers strongly opposed any entry of American troops, saying that the Republic had lost enough territory to its northern neighbor; should these troops come and decide to remain, there would be little that Mexico could do to evict them. Finally, on October 16, 1880—the day after Victorio's defeat—the Mexican President finally agreed to submit a border reciprocity agreement to his Senate. However, Díaz was merely stalling, for in reality he did not have to seek approval from anyone on such matters. Those American troops that did cross the international border in pursuit of Victorio did so illegally; moreover, those Mexican troops that crossed the border going north violated American territorial sovereignty.

Northern Mexico (present-day Sonora and Chihuahua). Victorio's last battleground.→

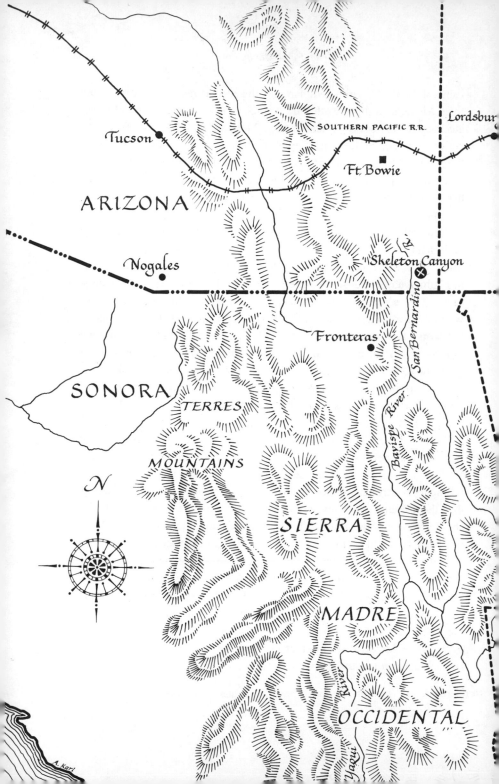

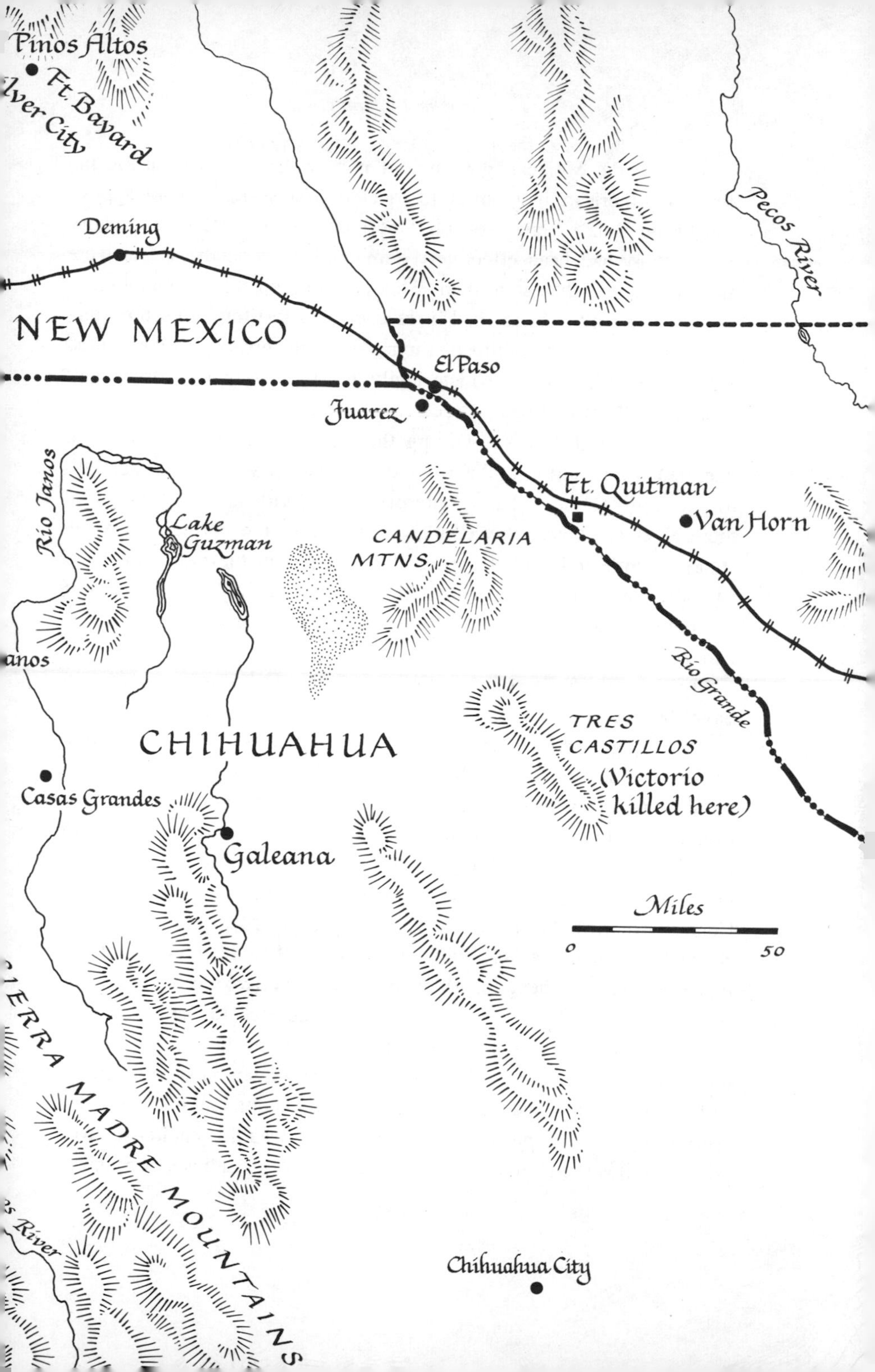
Pinos Altos
Ft. Bayard
lver City
Deming
NEW MEXICO
Pecos River
El Paso
Juarez
Rio Janos
Lake Guzman
CANDELARIA MTNS.
Ft. Quitman
Van Horn
anos
Rio Grande
CHIHUAHUA
TRES CASTILLOS
(Victorio killed here)
Casas Grandes
Galeana
Miles
0
50
SIERRA MADRE MOUNTAINS
s River
Chihuahua City

In truth, the Mexican government may well have been using the threat of American intervention to squelch the last remnants of opposition to the Díaz regime. Several times previously in Mexican history this strategy had been effectively employed by scoundrels who were more politicians than statesmen. This had worked well in many cases because the United States had in fact wrested territory from the Mexicans. The loss of one-third of their sovereign territory to the United States was still too close historically for most Mexicans to forget. Moreover, there had been a recurring theme of filibustering from the north for several decades. During the 1850's a number of men had departed from California determined to separate Sonora or Baja California from Mexico. These enterprising individuals had thought of themselves as Dukes, Presidents, or Sultans of the northern Mexican states. Significantly, filibustering still lingered in the minds of many Mexicans and a few Americans. And in 1880, reminding Mexicans of the potential danger of new filibustering expeditions was one Ernest Dalrymple.

Mysteriously financed, perhaps a crackpot, Dalrymple was said to have the backing of English and German merchants in Mexico who wanted to overthrow the government. These merchants feared growing Mexican economic ties with the United States. Such an alignment would interfere with their export-import business, and therefore they preferred to take over Mexico, thereby ending trade agreements with the United States. Dalrymple was a Pennsylvanian who, during 1880, called for an invasion of Mexico and an eventual occupation of all Central America. On February 7, 1880, he issued a proclamation in Santa Fe, requesting his fellow citizens to "behold a vision of enchantment, a continent lulled by the waves of two oceans slumbering." This would-be conqueror was also reported to have remarked that "undying glory crowns the knight whose daring arm unveils the dazzling future." He unfurled a blue flag with a sunburst as a symbol of his new country, and called for an army of occupation of 50,000 men who would be equipped by a syndicate of wealthy capitalists who wished to invest $15 million. In July Dalrymple grandiosely organized the states of California and Texas and the territories of Arizona and New Mexico into what he called the "Department of the Rio Grande," and announced himself as "General of the Occupation Army." [9]

This new "general" located his headquarters at Austin, Texas, appointed F. W. James another "general," and divided his as yet non-existent army into five corps. The one commanded by James was the First to be organized. He provided for the training of corps commanders and then set up a court-martial procedure for those who refused to obey his orders. Evidently, although he appeared a crank to many people and had no real chance for success, Dalrymple was very serious. He proceeded to organize his initial regiment of 300 men, calling it the First Regiment of Texas Cavalry. (Some estimates of the size of this regiment ranged as high as 700.) However, "General" James was also a member of the Texas militia, and when the Texas Governor heard of the new organization, he insisted that James resign one of his commissions. James thereupon abandoned Dalrymple; however, he reported that Dalrymple's army was real and that the "general" actually planned to enter Mexico. Little wonder that the Mexicans were concerned about American troops chasing Victorio on Mexican soil!

In addition to fears generated by Dalrymple's army, the Mexicans believed that revolutionaries under the leadership of one General Leonardo Márquez were organizing in the United States for an invasion of northern Mexico. In June 1880, Márquez was reported near Tucson, where he was supposedly recruiting. Colonel Eugene Carr's Sixth Cavalry stopped Márquez from entering Sonora, and he fled to Los Angeles, ultimately going to Baja California. In August, after being whipped by a loyal Mexican force, Márquez re-entered the United States by way of Arizona. Carr's troops were there, and they arrested the entire group. Although Márquez and Dalrymple failed, the Mexican authorities were wary of American intentions and involvement. [10]

Undoubtedly, the activities of these filibusters had much to do with

President Díaz' refusal to agree to border reciprocity. Dalrymple was never able to get his movement sufficiently organized, and it collapsed almost as quickly as it was born, while Marquez quietly disappeared from the scene.

Yet the Mexican authorities were sufficiently concerned with the Indian problem, as well as the threat of American intervention, to take action. During August hostiles had attacked the small village of Santa Rosa. Victorio was blamed for all the raids that occurred, although he was responsible for only a few of them. The Indians in the vicinity of Santa Rosa, a local tribe, had good reason to be angry with the citizens of that town, for the people there had duped them with a feast and then had arrested as many as possible and had sent them to Mexico City to prison. Before the transfer south could be accomplished, the Indians broke away, vowing to teach the citizens a lesson. Thus for several weeks, whenever troops were not present, the Indians attacked the people and the village.

Stories were rampant of how the sanguinary Indians dressed in Mexican clothes, stopped Mexican peasants, inquired whether they were from Santa Rosa, and if they were, killed them in the most horrible fashion. Despite the fact that some of the raids had not been committed by Victorio's band, the Mexicans were ready to try anything to stop them.[11]

Meanwhile, in New Mexico, Agent Russell, at the Mescalero Reservation, conceded in his report to the Indian Commissioner in July 1880 that acts of depredation were continuing all along the frontier. In fact, one group of five unidentified Indians approached a large herd of cattle, talked with the cowhands for a short while, and, when the cattle had been placed in the corral, killed several of the men and took two horses, a rifle, a pistol, some blankets, and other supplies. The victims were from the Mescalero Agency, and when the survivors returned to the reservation and reported the attack, a detachment of soldiers went to the grisly scene. They found one steer dead and the remainder of the herd scattered. The Indians had disappeared, leaving no sign of where they might have gone. The attacking Indians were probably from the Mescalero Reservation, but Russell said that they were renegades, part of a group that had at one time run with Victorio. From the descriptions given, Russell recognized some of the Indians, but he reported that they had not been on the reservation for several months. Reservation Indians, who were sometimes threatened by this group, made it clear to the Army that they wanted nothing to do with these "bad" Indians. There was so great a threat throughout the area, however, that the agent regarded it extremely dangerous to travel farther than three miles away from the reservation without the protection of troops.[12]

For several months the hard-pressed soldiers in New Mexico failed to control the Indians, and by the fall of 1880 it was common knowledge throughout the United States that the Army officers had more serious troubles in New Mexico than they were admitting. The *Boston Daily Advertiser* carried a short article describing the condition of the Army as miserable, for few soldiers were adequately supplied with horses; furthermore, the newspaper hinted that this was a result of the usual poor leadership of the Army command. However, as all local reports from New Mexico to Washington had to pass through Santa Fe and the government-owned telegraph, little concerning Indian raids and the inability of the Army to cope with the problem actually was known in the eastern section of the country.[13]

Permission to cross the Mexican border had been difficult to obtain, but by September 15, 1880, Colonel Terrazas and the Mexican authorities in Chihuahua evidently tired of waiting for federal permission for United States troops to cross the international line. These Mexicans gave limited crossing privileges to the Americans. Preparations were made and Captain Beyer, at El Paso, was told to stand ready to move West to the eastern Patrillo Mountains—a march he actually made at night, on September 23, 1880. Lieutenant James A. Maney of the Fifteenth Infantry, with twenty black troopers, was to move south into Mexico from near the Patrillo Mountains, while others would stop at Palomas Lake and Bocco Grande Pass, the day after Beyer's march. About September 15, 1880, several American Army columns crossed the

Rio Grande, heading for the Candalaría Mountains, the last known campsite of the Victorio band. Charles Berger, a white scout who had followed the hostiles with the help of two Indian scouts, reported that the Mexicans had stepped out of Victorio's way, letting the wily Apache head west. Each of these commands had scouts along to track the hostiles. George W. Baylor and his Texas Rangers also were given permission again to cross into Mexico, and southward they rode.

As Colonel George P. Buell led some of these men into Mexico, his real fear was that Victorio would slip northward through the net. Buell began his march about noon on September 21, taking along a supply train and a 400-gallon water wagon. Almost immediately after entering Mexico, Buell read in Victorio's actions signs that indicated that the Indians knew and were surprised that the Americans had crossed the border, for the Apaches immediately changed course and headed into the Candalaría Mountains. Most of the Army elements were in place, for only Colonel Eugene Carr and his men were not yet ready. Buell waited a full day at Guzman's Springs for Carr. As a precautionary move, however, he sent Captain Jack Crawford, chief of Indian scouts, toward the east, up to the Rio Grande—still fearing that the hostiles would double back north.

Unable to wait longer for Carr, Buell ordered Captain Beyer to head into the Candalaría Mountains, but a nervous sentry carelessly fired a random shot, spooking the horses and mules and leaving most of Beyer's command on foot. This action effectively removed Beyer's men from any quick pursuit. On the night of September 29 Buell led his men to the north end of the Candalaría Mountains. The Americans found almost no water. They realized how vulnerable to ambush they were in the excessively rough terrain. On October 1, Buell received a dispatch from General Terrazas, informing the Americans that Mexican troops had not arrived quickly enough to stop Victorio's southward movement. The hostiles had last been seen heading toward the Pine Mountains, to the southeast.

Buell received supplies from a United States Army wagon train on October 2, near El Lucero, and then moved on the Chihuahua Road to

Santa Recia, keeping his command north of Victorio. However, no one, Mexican or American, knew exactly where the skillful warrior was hiding. Buell sent Lieutenant James Maney, a few scouts, and one company of cavalry under Lieutenant Charles M. Schaeffer to join Terrazas at the Borracho, while Buell led the balance of the men down the Rio Grande Valley, remaining south of Fort Quitman, on the Mexican side of the border. On October 9, with Victorio still eluding both armies, Buell moved most of his troops to the Borracho. He had encamped at the Borracho and was resting his mounts and giving his men a few hours sleep when, at about eleven o'clock that evening, he received information from General Terrazas via Lieutenant Maney that it would be objectionable to the Mexican government if American troops remained longer in Mexico. Knowing he was in the country without federal sanctions, Buell on October 10 started the long, dry march back to the United States, convinced that Terrazas probably was acting on higher orders relating to the Americans.[14]

The Mexicans apparently gave this order hoping the hostiles would continue west, possibly re-entering the United States in Arizona. The Mexicans may even have had an agreement with the Apache leader that as long as the Indians did not attack major villages and haciendas they would be let alone. However, when the Chihuahuan government learned that the hostiles merely had taken up residence in the Corral de Piedras and were refusing to return to the United States, the authorities knew they had to take swift and decisive action.

Once in Mexico, Victorio had not been idle. He had attacked villages, killed isolated herders, and had made the entire frontier region unsafe for local citizens. He had raided Don Mariano Samaniego's ranch, stolen 117 horses and mules, killed two Mexican herders, and taken sanctuary in the mountains near by. In desperation, Don Ramón Arranda, leader of some Mexican volunteers, had asked the Texas Rangers to cooperate with them in bringing the Apaches to terms. On September 17, 1880, Lieutenant Baylor and fourteen Rangers had entered Mexico, marching to Arranda's ranch. There they had joined Mexican volunteers from the near-by towns, forming a combined force of over 100 men. The Rangers then discovered that the Indians were traveling south of the Ranchería Mountains, but the number of hostiles and their exact direction was not discernible—rain the night before had obliterated their trail. Moreover, before the Rangers and volunteers could track down the Apaches, the entire force was ordered by Mexican authorities to hold at the Ranchería Mountains, getting into position before Victorio could arrive. In short, these Tejanos were to wait for an opportunity to ambush the Apaches. After waiting impatiently for a short time, and learning that the hostiles were not traveling in their direction, this force moved on a night march toward El Cobre Mountains. During this march the group again encountered the hostiles' trail and learned that Victorio's entire band had crossed the Chihuahua stage road, evidently heading into the Candalaría Range. The volunteers thereupon marched to San José to await the arrival of General Joaquín Terrazas with Mexican troops.

Don Joaquín Terrazas was the man of the hour for Chihuahua. He knew well how to track and punish Apaches, and, even more significantly, he was willing to serve his region whenever called. Ranger James B. Gillett described Terrazas much as others have done. A member of a prominent family in Chihuahua, Terrazas was a charismatic leader, an impressive figure who stood more than six feet tall. Gillett said the Mexican patriot was "very dark, and an inveterate smoker of cigarettes." [15] Terrazas owned four milk-white horses; he rode one while his aides led the other three. Most of the Mexicans accompanying Terrazas were volunteers, armed with Remington pistols and carbines, but they appeared ready for battle; most of the infantrymen were Indians from the country, who wore rawhide sandals and were armed with Remington muskets. Each soldier carried two belts of ammunition. Terrazas had a total of some 400 fighting men.

It had not been easy for Terrazas to organize his men, for the age-old struggle between federalism and centralism had injected itself, causing difficulties between the federal troops sent to solve Indian problems and the volunteers led by the aggressive Terrazas. Political difficulties had begun very early in the Victorio campaign and, combined with recurring revolutionary outbreaks, had contributed to the Mexican failure to bring adequate pressure on the hostiles. In December 1879, Terrazas had marched to San Andres to meet Colonel Ponciano Cisneros with more than 100 of General Geronimo Treviño's troops. Terrazas had told Cisneros he had no aspirations to command and therefore would cooperate to the fullest extent to find the Apaches. After marching around the northern sections of Chihuahua for two months, the men had given up and returned to the capital city on February 5, 1880. Although the two leaders had cooperated to some extent during the campaign, under the surface there was disagreement—perhaps jealousy. After the return to Chihuahua City, Terrazas had decided to administer his private business and to lead volunteers against the Apaches only when necessary.

By the end of February 1880, Colonel Adolfo J. Valle, with a large contingent of federal troops, had arrived in Chihuahua for frontier duty. Valle sent out his scouts, but after several days of seeing nothing but mountains and deserts, they had returned empty-handed. Victorio was in the United States at this time. In June the Apache had led his band back to Mexico, camping in the Las Lagunas area. Valle had stalled for a short time—he claimed he was unable to strike the Indians at once—and by the end of the month had headed in the general area of the hostiles' camp. By this time the Apaches again were on the move; they soon returned to the United States. Valle had left his cavalry at Carrizal and most of his infantry at Hacienda del Carmen while he journeyed to Chihuahua for a brief rest.

By this time Governor Luis Terrazas had become very alarmed at the Apache successes, and he called Joaquín Terrazas and Adolfo Valle to his home for consultation. According to Terrazas, Colonel Valle was exceedingly stubborn, refusing to cooperate with local authorities. Governor Terrazas advised both men that he had raised money to pay the volunteers a token reward, and moreover that he had raised a 2000-peso reward to be paid to the man who killed Victorio. Valle was not interested in the reward; in fact he had refused to send his men back on the trail. This was in August of 1880, and Valle claimed that his men and their mounts were so exhausted that they were unable to continue. No agreement could be reached between the leaders, and they parted company somewhat annoyed at each other.

The following night the Governor called Joaquín Terrazas back to his house, and together they devised a plan that had possibilities of working. The Governor had spoken that day with the political chief of Guerrero and other regional caudillos who had volunteered men and ammunition for the Indian campaign. With plans made and supplies promised, Terrazas headed for San Andres on the morning of August 25, 1880, to obtain volunteers. The recruiting process proved slow, but after he visited several frontier villages, a number of men were raised.

The entire force visited Rebosadero Springs, about twenty miles south of El Chaparro, a location on the new Chihuahua stage road; they rested there two days before marching forty miles to Borracho Pass, the place where the Apaches had camped after killing General Byrnes and capturing Jesus Cota's stock. Twenty miles west of the Pass the Mexican force camped and awaited supplies. The Texas Rangers were by this time with the party, and when the supply wagon arrived, Terrazas allowed Baylor and the Rangers to draw ten days' rations for the expected march and fight.[16]

Gillett claimed that, while he was standing near a Mexican wagon, a Mexican soldier stole a fine hunting knife from his belt. He reported the loss to Baylor, who mentioned the episode to Terrazas. Terrazas tried to find the knife, but soon gave up. One year later, after the defeat of Victorio, one of Terrazas' aides appeared in the Ranger camp at Ysleta, handed the knife over to Gillett, and told him that the guilty party had been punished.

With supplies now in good order and enough men to move against Victorio, the combined force prepared to depart in the direction of the last known Indian camp. Before they could leave, and while still camped at Borracho, they were joined by a group of American troops that had crossed the border in pursuit of renegades. Lieutenant Charles M. Schaeffer, with part of the Ninth Cavalry, Lieutenant James Maney, Captain James Parker, and sixty-five Apache scouts, arrived to join the fight. Terrazas never quite trusted the Apache scouts because they were from Geronimo's band; the Mexican believed it would only be a matter of time before that group caused trouble. The Mexican general sent his own scouts out but allowed the Americans to work with them, hoping thereby to ascertain just where Victorio had gone. Scouting about seventy-five miles away from the camp, the Mexicans learned that the Apache chief once again had turned back southward, going deeper into the state of Chihuahua. Since this would take the Americans farther into Mexico, and since the general distrusted the Indian allies, he suggested to the Texas Rangers that they return to the United States. Thus the Rangers and the American soldiers were destined to miss the final fight.[17]

Terrazas believed he had Victorio cornered at last and therefore felt he needed no help from Americans. He sent word to Colonel Buell that the presence of the American troops was definitely objectionable to the Mexican authorities.[18] In fact, by this time, Terrazas knew approximately where the hostiles were and how many warriors they had in their group, and he did not intend to allow the Americans to enter into an affair that would perhaps give him an opportunity to destroy the hostiles once and for all, by which deed he could gain considerable popularity and influence in Mexico.[19]

It had been Colonel Buell's men who had crossed the border about September 15, and he who had continued to track Victorio until it was certain that the band had gone into the Candalaría Mountains. Likewise, it had been Buell who, on September 13, had sent couriers to Terrazas, telling him that the hostiles had been located. Buell also reported later that he understood that Colonel Baylor and his Rangers were actually with Terrazas at this time. Unfortunately, although he claimed to have been instrumental in finding Victorio, Buell was denied an opportunity to participate in the final fight with the Apaches. On his return, Buell praised his men and indicated that both officers and men had suffered considerably chasing the hostiles; their bravery should be officially recognized, the commander said.[20]

To Terrazas and his command fell the task of dealing with the hostiles. Victorio, with his main band of followers, had taken refuge in a range of hills called the Tres Castillos, about ninety-two miles north of Chihuahua City. Some disagreement still exists over just where Victorio and his band were camped. The Apaches may have been in a slight depression between two peaks, or they may have chosen to defend themselves on a single hill.

Terrazas and Juan Mata Ortiz, his second in command, divided their forces on October 12. Mata Ortiz led his party toward the Sierra de Tosesigua, carefully searching the terrain, while Terrazas marched his followers toward the llanos de los Castillos. Terrazas stayed in the saddle all night and arrived at the edge of the plains of Castillos at dawn on October 13. Terrazas knew where Victorio was, and he waited for the fast-riding Indians to cross between his two forces. Ultimately that occurred; in fact, Victorio camped at Tres Castillos, precisely between the two columns.[21]

Terrazas later explained his strategy. He said he knew he had Victorio trapped, and therefore he exposed only about twenty men, hoping Victorio would believe that to be the entire size of the pursuing force. Two kilometers away from the hostiles Terrazas prepared a formation change and then ordered his entire force to attack. It was later reported that the firing began at fifty paces, with the Tarahumara scout Mauricio el Corredor wounding Victorio in the first barrage.

Regardless of the details, the Mexicans caught up with the hostiles on October 14. The Apaches huddled in the rocks for protection during the night, while Mexican troops occupied positions from where they could open fire at sunrise. Firing commenced as the first streaks of dawn fell upon the mountains, and by 9 a.m. the battle was ended.

The Mexicans reported later that Victorio had been wounded several times, and after the battle, as he lay in considerable pain, Mauricio el Corredor walked up and shot him. Stories of Victorio's death varied considerably, but the Mexicans generally said it was a battle between the Apache chief and the Tarahumara scout, with Corredor winning. All told, Terrazas claimed that he and his men killed sixty-one braves and eighteen women and children, and that they had captured sixty women and children. About 120 horses, thirty-eight mules, and a couple of donkeys were also captured, along with many of the supplies and belongings of the Indians.[22]

Those Apaches who were captured were taken to different places in Chihuahua and made to work or live as the Mexicans did. The wounded Apaches were treated in hospitals, according to Mexican reports, and their children were placed in Mexican homes. It was said that two sons of Victorio, one fourteen, the other four, were in the captured group. The younger of the two was later baptized and named Victor Castellanos, so all would know he was Victorio's son, captured at Tres Castillos. After the Apaches agreed to make treaties with the Mexicans, they were given an opportunity to see him. According to Mexican legend he refused to go with his tribe and thus remained in Mexico. Later he was educated at a Catholic school. He died of tuberculosis at the age of seventeen.

Two New Mexican youths, Pirso Padilla and Cesaria Chávez, both members of extremely poor families, were liberated from Apache captivity as a result of the battle at Tres Castillos. While these captives could not immediately obtain passage back to New Mexico, eventually they were able to return to their homes.[23]

Although Victorio and most of his band were killed or captured in the engagement, some of his warriors were not in the camp, and they therefore escaped. Colonel Grierson reported, on October 30, 1880, that some of his men were attacked near Ojo Caliente. Thirty-five or more Apaches were in the assault, but no one was certain whether these were remnants of Victorio's band or renegades from the Mescalero Reservation. In this skirmish four soldiers died; there were wounded on both sides, but the numbers are not known.[24]

Before the heavy fighting began on October 15, 1880, some of Victorio's band was able to slip away during the night. One survivor, James Kaywaykla, who was at the time a small child, later told his impressions of the struggle. According to Kaywaykla a tribal council was held a few days before the final battle; in this the leaders of the tribe said that their situation was very bad. The Indians had been pursued for days, were short of food and ammunition, and badly needed rest. Kaywaykla recalled that all of the Apaches agreed that Nana would take some warriors and forage for supplies. Thus thirty warriors were gone when the Mexicans attacked. Kaywaykla claimed that, in addition to Nana's band, seventeen other Indians survived the massacre. After waiting for several days, these Apaches returned to Tres Castillos to bury the dead, who had been left in ghastly array there by the Mexicans. Finally, Kaywaykla said that the group buried Victorio's body with his own knife embedded in his heart—yet another version of the great warrior's death.

Indian depredations did not cease in New Mexico or Chihuahua with the demise of Victorio and his band. On November 16, 1880, Indians punished Mexicans for the killing of Victorio's band. Mexican troops traveling between Chihuahua and El Paso were ambushed and nine of them were killed. It was said that one of the Mexican sergeants was using Victorio's saddle and carrying a few trinkets from the body of the fallen Apache leader. The Indians displayed their displeasure with the Mexicans by mutilating the sergeant's body. For months thereafter the Mexicans continued to pay a grim price for having ended Victorio's career. Victorio's forces, joined at different times by as many as 250 Mescaleros, had created a formidable foe for the Mexican militia and the United States Army. The trail of blood these hostiles left eventually cost more than 400 Mexican and American lives.

News of Victorio's death reached various points in the United States within a couple of days. One report came from Doctor Mariano Samaniego of Paso del Norte, whose brother resided at Carrizal. A young officer in Terrazas' command told of the encounter, relating that the Indians were "caught like rats in a trap and unable to retreat. . . ." Many Mexicans realized that without the help of American troops, Terrazas could not have succeeded. The American troops had kept the hostiles from fleeing north again.[25]

The grateful citizens of Chihuahua gave the Mexican participants in the battle against Victorio a tricolor flag with an inscription in gold: "15 October 1880—Triumph over Victorio and his band, in Tres Castillas [sic]." [26] The people of Chihuahua also published a folder praising the men for their activities. The participants were received as heroes in Chihuahua City. As the Mexican troops paraded through the streets, gleeful citizens stood on the rooftops, seeking a glimpse of the fighting men. Bands played, bells rang, and gaily frocked señoritas were everywhere. Then the Mexican militia and regulars rode triumphantly through the streets, and the scalps of the fallen Apaches were waved at the people. Twenty-eight scalps, seventeen the scalps of women and children, were displayed. Victorio's slayer, Mauricio el Corredor, was given an ornate suit with a jacket of crimson broadcloth and vest and pants of black doeskin, all trimmed with silver lace, and a hat with a wide, white fur brim, covered with spangles. He also received other gifts from the Governor and the grateful populace. Mauricio told his exciting story of victory many times, and doubtless lost sight of any objectivity—perhaps lost sight of the truth.[27]

The people of northern Mexico were as grateful to see Victorio dead as were those who had been plagued by the attacks. In Hermosillo, Sonora, a town that was often itself attacked by different Indians, a newspaper editorial expressed the local sentiment. Calling Victorio a terrible scourge of the country, the editor reminded his readers that Victorio's influence had been far-reaching, causing other hostiles to attack settlements. As in Chihuahua, so in Sonora—the citizens applauded the bravery and success of the militia and the regular army.[28]

8
CONCLUSION

Conflict is the word which best describes the era in which the United States Army so doggedly pursued Victorio and the Ojo Caliente Apaches in New Mexico and Chihuahua. The Lincoln County War, in which Billy the Kid gained his notoriety, pitted politician against merchant and merchant against cattleman as all vied for economic and political power. The white frontiersmen, who settled there bitterly disagreed with the actions of the soldiers, as well as with those of the Indian agents, while the Army officers and representatives of the Indian Bureau contended for control over the reservations.

Within the Army there was the conflict of black versus white that saw the buffalo soldiers of the Ninth and Tenth Cavalry seeking parity with the men in other regiments, while Army officers who had been graduated from the Military Academy at West Point looked down upon those officers who had risen through the ranks. Colonel Eugene A. Carr, a graduate of the Academy, looked with considerable disdain on Benjamin Grierson and others who had come up through the ranks. Carr likewise looked down upon officers who commanded blacks.

Yet another major conflict in New Mexico at this time was that between the residents of Latin-American ancestry and the Anglo-Americans; pioneering whites saw the Hispanos, as they sometimes were called, as lazy, backward, image-worshipping Catholics, while

180

the Latins saw the newcomers as greedy, grasping robbers. "Gringo" and "Greaser" were among the more polite of the epithets they hurled at one another. And this conflict between the Hispanos and the Anglos carried over into relationships between Americans and Mexicans; there was rancor and hatred on both sides of the international boundary. Moreover, there even was conflict between the Mexicans themselves as one revolution after another swept the country, each bringing with it death and destruction.

And overshadowing all these conflicts was the one between the red men and the whites, as the Anglo-American newcomers refused to recognize the alternate lifestyle of the native Americans—and even reacted violently to the Indian desire to remain even partially Indian. The Bureau of Indian Affairs at this time was committed philosophically to making these original owners of the land "take the white man's road," as the agents on the various reservations tried to force the Indians from their old pattern of life into a new one of farming and ranching.

Because of all these problems, it was little wonder that many contemporary observers considered the swirling currents of conflict to be insoluble. In the end, one problem after another either solved itself or else died of old age, but it is astonishing that there was any kind of order during this period, rather than that there was so much disorder. The price of peace in the 1870's and 1880's was paid largely by the Indians and blacks rather than by the whites; both these groups would remain outside the mainstream of American life despite the blood they shed and the property that was destroyed. Both Indians and Negroes served their country's purposes, but when the wars ended neither race had anything to celebrate.

There was no great victor in the Victorio campaign—certainly neither the Army nor the white residents of New Mexico gained much by it—for at the end even the whites were left with nothing to celebrate. The Indians had been corraled and their land opened to settlement, but the end of the war saw the soldiers withdrawn and, with their withdrawal, the beginning of an economic depression.

Victorio and his band of Ojo Caliente Apaches ultimately were defeated, most of them dying, but a few going to the reservations as virtual prisoners of war. The tragedy of this band was but part of the larger tragedy of all the American Indians during the same period. In 1871 there were an estimated 321,000 Indians in the United States; by 1885 this number had declined to 260,000, most of them penned up on reservations, out of the path of the expanding white civilization. The cause of the recurring hostilities between the two races was never faced realistically, and neither side ever sought a peaceful resolution to their underlying differences. Even now there is no agreement as to a proper resolution to the conflict—which goes on today as an open clash of philosophies rather than as a clash of arms.

The reasons why no one in the post-Civil War period sought a compromise acceptable both to Indians and whites are complicated. One strong factor was the nature of American society as it emerged from the war. Between 1861 and 1865 the nation had engaged in a life-and-death struggle. When the war ended, Americans had no time to consider the problems of Indians living on the periphery of white civilization, for there yet were serious by-products of the Civil War to divert the nation's attention. The politics of Reconstruction, an unprecedented industrial growth, the building and development of the railroads, the enjoyment of peace and prosperity, and finally an economic panic from 1873 to 1879; all diverted the best minds of that era away from the Indian problem. Moreover, this rapid change and economic expansion brought a widespread dislocation of people, perhaps causing some frustrations. In the reconstructed South, that frustration could be turned against blacks, while along the fringes of settlement the Indian was a scapegoat for white aggression.

Meanwhile, there were tensions that prompted several Indian tribes to maintain a warlike attitude. No clear governmental policy was employed; the various federal departments dealing with the Indians vacillated. The Indians, therefore, never knew what to expect from government officials. In the Territory of New Mexico, individuals seeking to establish economic hegemonies clearly broke the law, as was the case in the Lincoln County War. The efforts made by whites to dupe Indians or to incite them against other whites was another factor causing trouble. Moreover, the activities of the scalp hunters might have prompted the hostiles to "fight fire with fire" and commit atrocities. These actions doubtless led the Indians to believe that if the whites dealing with each other and the Indians were corrupt, then the Indians should not allow themselves to be quietly disposed of or removed from lands they had inhabited for centuries.

Many of these conflicts could have had considerable influence on the conduct of the Indian war against Victorio. Nothing really was solved by the fighting, beyond the reduction of the number of Indians, and eventually the relegation of Indians to reservations. Victorio repeatedly stated that he wanted only to be let alone to live on centuries-old tribal lands near Ojo Caliente, New Mexico. What he meant, in reality, was that he wanted to be Indian and he wanted to accept American help on this reservation, but he simultaneously wanted to retain a measure of self-determination. Such today is the cry of the militant descendants of these brave warriors: "Give us self-determination without termination." They want to run their own affairs, remain Indian, and not have their lifestyle or opportunities limited because they are Indian. Apparently the Victorio campaign accomplished nothing, other than proving that violence only begets counter-violence, and that an American minority through violence cannot gain the right to self-determination. Reason, not force, must prevail, else Indian and white will return to an appeal to force—a tactic which failed Victorio and his followers and brought bloodshed and destruction in its wake.

NOTES

CHAPTER I

[1] Several studies are available which detail the problems the Spanish government had with Indians. See Max L. Moorhead, *The Apache Frontier; Jacobo Ugarte and Spanish–Indian Relations in Northern New Spain, 1769–1791* (Norman: University of Oklahoma Press, 1968); Jack Forbes, *Apache, Navajo, and Spaniard* (Norman: University of Oklahoma Press, 1960); Sidney B. Brinkerhoff and Odie B. Faulk, *Lancers for the King* (Phoenix: Arizona Historical Foundation, 1965); Edward H. Spicer, *Cycles of Conquest: The Impact of Spain, Mexico, and the United States on the Indians of the Southwest* (Tucson: University of Arizona Press, 1962); Charles L. Kenner, *A History of New-Mexican–Plains-Indian Relations* (Norman: University of Oklahoma Press, 1969). For information concerning the end of Spanish rule see Hugh M. Hamill, Jr., *The Hidalgo Revolt: Prelude to Mexican Independence* (Gainesville: University of Florida Press, 1966).

[2] For General Carasco's remarks concerning Apaches see John C. Cremony, *Life Among the Apaches* (Glorietta, N.M.: Rio Grande Press, 1868 reprinted), 38, 39, 41; Joseph A. Stout, Jr., *The Liberators: Filibustering Expeditions into Mexico 1848–1862 and the Last Thrust of Manifest Destiny* (Los Angeles: Westernlore, 1973), 20, 37–38. For general Mexican frontier conditions see Fernando Jordán, *Crónica de un Pais Bárbaro*, 2nd ed. (Mexico: Talleres De B. Costa-Amic, 1965); and Francisco R. Almada, *Resumen de Historia del Estado de Chihuahua* (Mexico: Libros Mexicanos, 1955).

[3] For these colonization plans see Odie B. Faulk (ed.), "Projected Mexican Military Colonies for the Borderlands, 1848," *Journal of Arizona History*, X (Spring 1968), 39–47; Mariano Paredes, *Projectos de leyes sobra colonización y comercio en el estado de Sonora, presentados a la Camara de Diputados por el representante de Aquel estado, en la sesión extraordinario del día 1850* (Mexico, D.F.: Ignacio Cumplido, 1850); Odie B. Faulk (ed.), "A Colonization Plan for Northern Sonora, 1850," *New Mexico Historical Review*, XLIV (Oct. 1969), 293–314; Odie B. Faulk (ed.), "Projected Mexican Colo-

nies in the Borderlands, 1852," *Journal of Arizona History*, X (Summer 1969), 115–28; and Patricia R. Herring, "A Plan for the Colonization of Sonora's Northern Frontier: The Paredes Proyectos of 1850," *Journal of Arizona History*, X (Summer 1969), 115–28.

[4] For scalp hunting, especially in Chihuahua, and the activities of James Kirker see Ralph A. Smith, "Apache Plunder Trails Southward, 1831–1840, *New Mexico Historical Review*, XXXVII (Jan. 1962), 20–42; Ralph A. Smith, "Apache 'Ranching' Below the Gila, 1841–1845," *Arizoniana*, III (Winter 1962), 1–17; Ralph A. Smith, "The Scalp Hunter in the Borderlands 1835–1850," *Arizona and the West*, VI (Spring 1964), 5–22; Ralph A. Smith, "The Scalp Hunt in Chihuahua—1849," *New Mexico Historical Review*, XL (April 1965), 116–40; see also Ray Brandes, "Don Santiago Kirker, King of the Scalp Hunters," *Smoke Signal* (Fall 1962), 2–8.

[5] For an example of John J. Glanton's activities see Ralph A. Smith, "John Joel Glanton, Lord of the Scalp Range," *Smoke Signal* (Fall 1962), 9–16; see also Stout, *The Liberators*, 39–41; for an earlier work see Reid Mayne, *The Scalp Hunters: A Romance of Northern Mexico* (Philadelphia: Lippincott, 1851).

[6] For general information about state problems see Hubert Howe Bancroft, *History of the North Mexican States and Texas*, 2 vols. (San Francisco: History Co., 1884–1889), II; Ralph Roeder, *Juárez and His Mexico*, 2 vols. (New York: Greenwood, 1947, 1968).

[7] The Díaz regime, its relationship with the United States, and its effect upon Mexican political development are discussed in the following works: Daniel Cosío Villegas, *The United States Versus Porfirio Díaz*, trans. Nettie L. Bensen (Lincoln: University of Nebraska Press, 1963); Stanley R. Ross, *Francisco I. Madero, Apostle of Mexican Democracy* (New York: AMS Press, 1955, reprinted 1970); John K. Turner, *Barbarous Mexico*, new ed. (Austin: University of Texas Press, 1969).

CHAPTER II

[1] Some information concerning attitudes toward the Treaty of Guadalupe Hidalgo can be found in Ambrose H. Sevier and Nathan Clifford to James Buchanan, Querétaro, May 25, 1848, *House Exec. Doc.* 50, 30th Cong., 2nd sess., Serial 541, pp. 74–76. For information about James S. Calhoun see Ralph E. Twitchell, *The Leading Facts of New Mexican History*, 5 vols. (Cedar Rapids: Torch Press, 1912), II, pp. 270, 277, 282, 283, 293.

[2] A description of Mangas Coloradas and information about his death can be found in Daniel E. Conner, *Joseph Reddeford Walker and the Arizona Adventure*, ed. Donald J. Berthrong and Odessa Davenport (Norman: University of Oklahoma Press, 1956), 35–36.

[3] For information concerning Indian treatment see John P. Clum, "Apache Misrule," *New Mexico Historical Review*, V (April 1930), 138–53; V (July 1930), 221–39.

[4] See Dan L. Thrapp, *The Conquest of Apacheria* (Norman: University of Oklahoma Press, 1967), 13–14; see also Frank C. Lockwood, *The Apache Indians* (New York: Macmillan, 1938), 100–130.

[5] Robert M. Utley, "The Bascom Affair: A Reconstruction," *Arizona and the West,* III (Spring 1961), 59–68; Benjamin Sacks, "New Evidence on the Bascom Affair," *Arizona and the West,* IV (Autumn 1962), 261–78; Arthur H. Woodward, "Side Lights on Fifty Years of Apache Warfare, 1836–1886," *Arizoniana,* II (Fall 1961), 3–14; Ralph H. Ogle, *Federal Control of the Western Apaches: 1848–1886* (Albuquerque: University of New Mexico Press, 1940).

[6] Frank D. Reeve, "The Federal Indian Policy In New Mexico, 1858–1880" (4 parts), *New Mexico Historical Review,* XII (July 1937), 218–69; XIII (Jan. 1938), 14–62; XIII (April 1938), 146–91; XIII (July 1938), 261–313.

[7] *The War of the Rebellion: A Compilation of the Official Records of the Union and Confederate Armies,* 128 vols. (Washington, D.C.: G.P.O., 1880–1901), Series I, L, Part 1, p. 942; see also George W. Baylor, *John Robert Baylor: Confederate Governor of Arizona,* ed. Odie B. Faulk (Tucson: Arizona Historical Society, 1966), and Hubert Howe Bancroft, *History of Arizona and New Mexico, 1530–1888,* XVII (San Francisco: History Co., 1889).

[8] Conner, *Joseph Reddeford Walker,* p. 39.

[9] For Grant's policy see Lawrie Tatum, *Our Red Brothers and the Peace Policy of President Ulysses S. Grant* (Lincoln: University of Nebraska Press, 1971); see also Ogle, *Federal Control of Western Apaches 1848–1886.*

[10] James R. Hastings, "The Tragedy of Camp Grant in 1871," *Arizona and the West,* I (Summer 1959), 146–60; Jay J. Wagoner, *Arizona Territory 1863–1912: A Political History* (Tucson: University of Arizona Press, 1970), 126–32.

[11] Francis Heitman, *Historical Register and Dictionary of the United States Army, from Its Organization, September 29, 1789, to March 2, 1903,* 2 vols. (Urbana: University of Illinois Press, 1965), I, 340; see also George Crook, *Résumé of Operations Against Apache Indians, 1882–1886* (Washington, D.C., G.P.O., 1887); John G. Bourke, *On the Border with Crook* (New York: Greenwood, 1891, and reprints); George Crook, *General George Crook: His Autobiography,* ed. Martin F. Schmitt (Norman: University of Oklahoma Press, 1946).

[12] For information about Cochise see Barbara A. Tyler, "Cochise: Apache War Leader," *Journal of Arizona History,* VI (Spring 1965), 1–10; for Howard see Heitman, *Historical Register,* 546–47; Oliver O. Howard, *My Life and Experience Among Our Hostile Indians* (Hartford: N. D. Worthington, 1907).

[13] John Clum expressed his beliefs about the Apaches after he resigned as agent. See John P. Clum, "Apache Misrule," *New Mexico Historical Review,* V (April, July 1930); "Geronimo," *New Mexico Historical Review,* III (Jan., April, July 1928); "Victorio," *Arizona Historical Review,* II (Jan. 1930).

[14] For information about New Mexico forts see Andy Gregg, *Drums of Yesterday: The Facts of New Mexico* (Santa Fe: Press of the Territories, 1971).

[15] See Reeve, "Federal Indian Policy," 261–313.

[16] Angry outcries from New Mexican citizens can be found in any newspaper of the time. See esp. *Weekly New Mexican* (Santa Fe), May 7, 17, 1869.

[17] See esp. Silver City *Herald,* Sept. 27, 1879; this is representative of local feeling throughout the period.

[18] Information about the Lincoln County War can be found in William A. Keleher, *Violence in Lincoln County, 1869–1881* (Albuquerque: University of New Mexico Press, 1967); Maurice Garland Fulton, *History of the Lincoln County War,* ed. Robert N. Mullin (Tucson: University of Arizona Press, 1968).

[19] Lew Wallace, *An Autobiography,* 2 vols. (New York: Somerset, 1906).

[20] For Clum's account see John P. Clum, "The Apaches," *New Mexico Historical Review,* IV (April 1929), 107–27.

CHAPTER III

[1] The best work describing the United States Army in the post-Civil War era is Don Rickey, Jr., *Forty Miles a Day on Beans and Hay: The Enlisted Soldier Fighting the Indian Wars* (Norman: University of Oklahoma Press, 1962). See also James S. Hutchins, "Mounted Riflemen: The Real Role of Cavalry in the Indian Wars," *El Palacio,* 69 (Summer 1962), 85–91; Fairfax Downey, *Indian-fighting Army* (New York: Scribner's, 1941); and Richard Wormser, *The Yellowlegs: The Story of the United States Cavalry* (New York: Doubleday, 1966).

[2] Medical problems were generally recorded in *Records of the War Department, Adjutant General's Office, Record Group 94;* Post Returns 1879–1880 for Fort Davis, Fort Sill, Fort Concho, and Fort Bayard. See also P. M. Ashburn, *A History of the Medical Department of the United States Army* (Boston: Houghton-Mifflin, 1929).

[3] For information on blacks in the Army see William H. Leckie, *The Buffalo Soldiers: A Narrative of the Negro Cavalry in the West* (Norman: University of Oklahoma Press, 1967); Benjamin Quarles, *The Negro in the Civil War* (Boston: Little, Brown, 1953); L. D. Reddick, "The Negro Policy of the United States Army," *Journal of Negro History,* XXXIV (Jan. 1949), 14–15; Major E. L. N. Glass (comp. and ed.), *The History of the Tenth Cavalry, 1866–1921* (Tucson: Acme Printing, 1921).

[4] Heitman, *Historical Register,* I, 510.

[5] Frank M. Temple, "Colonel Grierson in the Southwest," *Panhandle Plains Historical Review,* 30 (1957), 27–54. Heitman, *Historical Register,* 478.

[6] Heitman, *Historical Register,* 729.

[7] For information about Flipper see Henry Ossian Flipper, *The Colored Cadet at West Point* (New York: H. Lee, 1878); see also *The Negro Frontiersman* (El Paso: Texas Western College Press, 1963); J. Norman Heard, *The Black Frontiersmen: Adventures of Negroes Among American Indians 1528–1918* (New York: John Day, 1969); Bruce J. Dinges, "The Court-Martial of Lieutenant Henry O. Flipper: An Example of Black-White Relations in the Army, 1881," *American West,* IX (Jan. 1972), 12–61; Heitman, *Historical Register,* 425.

[8] Robert M. Utley, *Fort Davis National Historic Site, Texas* (Washington, D.C.: National Park Service Historical Handbook, Series No. 38, 1965); Erwin N. Thompson,

"The Negro Soldiers on the Frontier: A Fort Davis Case Study," *Journal of the West,* VII (April 1968), 217–35; and esp. Major John Bigelow, Jr., *Tenth United States Cavalry, Historical Sketch, 1866–1892,* United States Army Commands, RG 98, National Archives. See also Colonel H. B. Wharfield, *10th Cavalry and Border Fights* (El Cajon, Calif.: privately printed, 1965).

[9] For information about Forts Sill and Gibson see Grant Foreman, *Fort Gibson: A Brief History* (Norman: University of Oklahoma Press, 1943); Wilbur S. Nye, *Carbine & Lance: The Story of Old Fort Sill* (Norman: University of Oklahoma Press, 1969).

[10] For general frontier conditions see Bancroft, *History of the North Mexican States and Texas;* see also Leckie, *Buffalo Soldiers,* 106–7; J. Evetts Haley, *Fort Concho and the Texas Frontier* (San Angelo, Tex.: San Angelo Standard Times, 1952).

[11] These difficulties were discussed each year in the *Annual Report of the Secretary of War for the Years 1866–1891;* border-crossing difficulties and negotiations can be found in *United States Department of State, Despatches from U. S. Ministers to Mexico, 1823–1906,* Record Group 59, National Archives. Hereafter cited as *Diplomatic Despatches.*

[12] *House Exec. Doc.* No. 1, Part 2, 45 Cong., 3 sess., 32, 33.

CHAPTER IV

[1] See Manuel Romero, "Victor el Apache que creo mi madre era hijo del gran jefe de los Apaches 'Victorio,' " *Boletín de la Sociedad Chihuahuense de Estudios Históricos,* IV (Jan.–Feb. 1944), 509–13; see also José Carlos Chávez, "Extinción de los Apaches," *Boletín de la Sociedad Chihuahuense de Estudios Históricos,* I (April 1939), 336–77.

[2] See Reeve, "Federal Indian Policy in New Mexico," part IV, 261–313; see also Ogle, *Federal Control of Western Apaches,* 184–96.

[3] Charles B. Gatewood, "Campaigning Against Victorio in 1879," *Great Divide* (April 1894) 102; see also Thomas Cruse, *Apache Days and After* (Caldwell, Ida., Caxton Press, 1941), 70–77.

[4] The best primary source detailing the activities of the Army in the Victorio campaign can be found in United States Government, National Archives and Record Service, Selected Documents Relating to the Activities of the Ninth and Tenth Cavalry in the Campaign Against Victorio, 1879–1880, Adjutant General's Office, Letters Received, File 6058-1879, Record Group 94. Hereafter cited as *Victorio File.*

[5] Information concerning the Mexican involvement in the Victorio campaign is incomplete. The Terrazas family left letters and documents of their vast endeavors in Chihuahua, but the best source is D. Joaquin Terrazas, *Memorias* (Juárez: Imprinta de "El Agricultor Mexicano" Escobar Hnos, 1905). Hereafter cited as Terrazas, *Memorias.*

[6] Indian accounts made during the great Indian wars do not exist. However, efforts have been made in recent years to gather oral accounts from Indians. These accounts shed some light on the sufferings and attitudes of the Indians, but doubtless must be used cautiously. See Eve Ball (ed.), *In the Days of Victorio: Recollections of a Warm Springs Apache,* narr. James Kaywaykla (Tucson: University of Arizona Press, 1970); see

also Eve Ball, "The Apache Scouts, A Chiricahua Appraisal," *Arizona and the West,* VII (Winter 1965), 315–28.

[7] *San Antonio Express,* March 19, 1879.

[8] *Ibid.* April 22, 1879.

[9] Santa Fe *Weekly New Mexican,* May 17, 1879.

[10] Santa Fe *Weekly New Mexican,* June 7, 1879.

[11] *San Antonio Express,* June 18, 1879.

[12] *Ibid.* July 16, 1879.

[13] *Ibid.* Aug. 14, 1879.

[14] Las Cruces *Thirty-Four,* Aug. 20, 1879.

[15] *Ibid.* Aug. 27, 1879; Russell also wrote a letter to the paper, and it is included in this issue.

[16] Governor Lewis Wallace to William McCrary, Santa Fe, Sept. 17, 1879, *Victorio File.*

[17] McCrary to Wallace, Washington, D.C., Sept. 18, 1879, *ibid.*

[18] Las Cruces *Thirty-Four,* Sept. 17, 1879.

[19] General E. D. Townsend to General John Pope, Washington, D.C., Sept. 18, 1879, *Victorio File.* Townsend was AG from February 22, 1869, to June 15, 1880, and therefore some correspondence was addressed to him by name, while other materials were addressed to the office.

[20] Heitman, *Historical Register,* 798.

[21] Pope to Townsend, Fort Leavenworth, Kans., Sept. 18, 1879, *Victorio File.*

[22] Gatewood, *Great Divide,* 102.

[23] Las Cruces *Thirty-Four,* Sept. 31, 1879.

[24] *Ibid.* Sept. 17, 1879.

[25] General Irvin McDowell to AG, San Francisco, Calif., Sept. 25, 1879, *Victorio File.*

[26] Gatewood, *Great Divide,* 102.

[27] *Ibid.*

[28] *Ibid.*

[29] *Ibid.*

[30] General P. H. Sheridan to AG, Chicago, Ill., Oct. 8, 1879; see also Colonel Edward Hatch to AG, Whipple Barracks, Ariz., Oct. 7, 1879; both *Victorio File.*

[31] *San Antonio Express,* Feb. 13, 1879.

[32] *Ibid.* Oct. 17, 19, 1879.

[33] Wallace to Territorial Legislature, 1880, Interior Department Territorial Papers, New Mexico, 1851–1914, Executive Proceedings, Oct. 8, 1774–Dec. 31, 1888, p. 1, National Archives Microcopy 364. Hereafter cited as Interior Department Papers.

[34] Pope to Sheridan, Oct. 16, 1879, *Victorio File.*

[35] *San Antonio Express,* Oct. 7, 1879.

[36] Santa Fe *Weekly New Mexican,* Oct. 4, 1879.

[37] *Ibid.*

[38] Governor Samuel Axtell to Territorial Legislature, 1880, Interior Department Papers, p. 7.

[39] Santa Fe *Weekly New Mexican,* Oct. 11, 1879.

[40] Pope to Sheridan, Fort Leavenworth, Kans., Nov. 4, 1879; *Victorio File.*

[41] Major Albert P. Morrow to AAG, District of New Mexico, Nov. 5, 1879, *ibid.*

[42] Gatewood, *Great Divide,* 103.

[43] *Ibid.*

[44] *Ibid.* 104.

CHAPTER V

[1] For information on Baylor and the Rangers chasing Victorio see Walter P. Webb, *The Texas Rangers: A Century of Frontier Defense* (Boston: Houghton-Mifflin, 1935); see also James B. Gillett, *The Texas Ranger: A Story of the Southwestern Frontier* (Chicago: World Book Co., 1927); and Gillett, *Six Years with the Texas Rangers* (New Haven: Yale University Press, 1925).

[2] *San Antonio Express,* Oct. 24, 1879.

[3] *Ibid.* Oct. 25, 1879.

[4] *Ibid.*

[5] William Evarts to Alexander Ramsey, Washington, D.C., June 28, 1880, *Victorio File;* for biographical information on Terrazas see *Diccionario Porrua de Historia, Biografía y Geografía de Mexico,* 2nd ed. (Mexico, D.F.: Editorial Porrua, 1964), 1566.

[6] *San Antonio Express,* Dec. 20, 1879.

[7] Las Cruces *Thirty-Four,* Jan. 7, 1880.

[8] Pope to AAG, Fort Leavenworth, Kans., Jan. 9, 1880, *Victorio File.*

[9] Las Cruces *Thirty-Four,* Jan. 14, 1880.

[10] *Ibid.* See also Morrow to AAAG, Fort Bayard, Nov. 5, 1880, *Victorio File.*

[11] Morrow to AG, Cañada Alamosa, Jan. 20, 1880, *ibid.*

[12] Santa Fe *Weekly New Mexican,* Jan. 17, 24, 1880.

[13] *Ibid.* Jan. 31, 1880.

[14] *Ibid.* Jan. 7, 1880.

[15] *Ibid.* Feb. 7, 1880.

[16] Hatch to AAG, Ojo Caliente, Feb. 25, 1880, *Victorio File.*

[17] Secretary of Interior to Secretary of War, Washington, D.C., Feb. 11, 1880, *ibid.*

[18] Pope to General W. T. Sherman, Fort Leavenworth, Kans., March 25, 1880, *ibid.*

[19] E. Montoya to W. G. Ritch (Acting Governor of New Mexico), San Antonio, March 23, 1880, *ibid.*

[20] Santa Fe *Weekly New Mexican,* April 5, 1880.

[21] *Ibid.* Nov. 29, 1879.

[22] *Ibid.* May 17, 1880.

[23] *Ibid.* April 5, 1880.

[24] Las Cruces *Thirty-Four,* April 21, 1880.

[25] Pope to AAG, Fort Leavenworth, Kans., April 13, 1880, *Victorio File;* see also Santa Fe *Weekly New Mexican,* April 12, 1880.

[26] Captain C. B. McLellan to Post Adjutant, Fort Bowie, May 16, 1880, *ibid.*

[27] Sheridan to AG, Washington, D.C., April 10, 1880, *ibid.* While most of the correspondence noted in this work gives specifics about Victorio, information listing battles can be found in *Record of Engagements with Hostile Indians Within the Military Division of the Missouri, from 1868 to 1882,* compiled from official records, Washington, D.C., G.P.O., 1882.

CHAPTER VI

[1] S. A. Russell to Commissioner of Indian Affairs, Mescalero Agency, N.M., March 27, 1880, *Victorio File.*

[2] W. G. Ritch to L. & H. Huning, Las Lunes, N.M., April 3, 1880, *ibid.;* see also Santa Fe *Weekly New Mexican,* April 12, 1880.

[3] Sheridan to Townsend, Chicago, April 16, 20, 1880, with endorsements, *ibid.*

[4] Colonel Benjamin Grierson to AAG, Department of Texas, Fort Davis, May 9, 1880, *ibid.;* see also Santa Fe *Weekly New Mexican,* May 10, 24, 1880; see also Frank M. Temple, "Colonel B. H. Grierson's Victorio Campaign," *West Texas Historical Association Yearbook,* XXXV (Oct. 1959), 99–111.

[5] Pope to AAG, Fort Leavenworth, Kans., April 28, 1880, *ibid.*

[6] Santa Fe *Weekly New Mexican,* May 10, 24, 1880.

[7] Silver City *Herald,* May 22, 1880.

[8] Silver City *Grant County Herald,* June 12, 1880.

[9] Cimarron *The News and Press,* Nov. 27, 1879.

[10] G. W. Bailey to R. B. Hayes, Silver City, May 10, 1880, *Victorio File.*

[11] U. S. Department of the Interior, *Report of the Commissioner of Indian Affairs, 1880,* p. 7. Hereafter cited as *Interior Department Report.*

[12] Sheridan to Townsend, Chicago, May 22, 1880, *Victorio File.*

[13] Adna R. Chaffee to Commissioner of Indian Affairs, San Carlos, Ariz., May 11, 1880, *ibid.*

[14] Pope to AAG, Fort Leavenworth, Kans., May 20, 1880, *ibid.*

[15] *Ibid.* May 5, 1880.

[16] For example, see newspaper clippings of Silver City *Daily Southwest;* see also W. A. Bennett to Governor of New Mexico, Santa Fe, May 16, 1880, both *ibid.*

[17] *Interior Department Report,* p. 7.

[18] Silver City *Daily Southwest,* May 5, 6, 1880, *Victorio File.*

[19] Simon Kropp, ''Albert J. Fountain and the Fight for Public Education in New Mexico, *Arizona and the West,* II (Winter 1969), 341–58.

[20] Las Cruces *Thirty-Four,* April 28, 1880.

[21] Reprinted in Cimarron *News and Press,* April 15, 1880.

[22] Santa Fe *Weekly New Mexican,* May 30, 1880.

[23] Sheridan to Townsend, Chicago, May 27, 1880, *Victorio File.*

[24] *Ibid.*

[25] Pope to AAG, Fort Leavenworth, Kans., June 2, 1880, *ibid.*

[26] S. M. Ashenfelter to Secretary of War, Silver City, June 4, 1880, *ibid.*

[27] *Socorro Sun,* Aug. 7, 1880.

[28] Santa Fe *Weekly New Mexican,* June 7, 1880.

[29] Sheridan to Townsend, Chicago, June 8, 1880, *Victorio File.*

[30] Pope to AAG, Fort Leavenworth, Kans., June 5, 1880, *ibid.*

[31] Chávez, ''Extinción de los Apaches,'' 336.

[32] *Ibid.* 337; see also *Diccionario Porrua,* 1566.

[33] Chávez, ''Extinción de los Apaches,'' 337, 346; see also Terrazas, *Memorias,* 69–81. For earlier information about the situation in Chihuahua see Robert Sandels, ''Silvestre Terrazas and the Old Regime in Chihuahua,'' *Américas* 28 (Oct. 1971), 191–205.

[34] Pope to AAG, Fort Leavenworth, Kans., June 14, 1880, *Victorio File.*

[35] Hatch to AAG, Santa Fe, Aug. 23, 1880, *ibid.*

[36] Russell to Commissioner of Indian Affairs, March 27, 1880, *ibid.*

[37] G. W. Smith to Post Adjutant, Tulerosa, N.M., Nov. 17, 1879, *ibid.*

[38] Pope to AAG, Fort Leavenworth, Kans., June 16, 1880, *ibid.*

[39] Santa Fe *Weekly New Mexican,* July 5, 1880.

[40] D. Madden to Post AG, Fort Bowie, Ariz., June 2, 1880, *Victorio File.*

[41] Russell to Commissioner of Indian Affairs, Mescalero Agency, N.M., June 10, 1880, *ibid.*

[42] St. Louis *Republican,* June 25, 1880, *ibid.*

[43] *San Antonio Express,* July 30, 1880.

[44] Sheridan to AG, Chicago, July 20, 1880, *Victorio File.*

[45] Sheridan to AG, Chicago, July 22, 1880, *ibid.*

[46] E. O. C. Ord to AG, San Antonio, Tex., July 24, 1880, *ibid.*

[47] Sheridan to AG, Chicago, Aug. 2, 1880, *ibid.*

[48] *San Antonio Express,* Aug. 2, 1880.

[49] Ord to AG, San Antonio, Aug. 4, 1880, *Victorio File.*

[50] AAG, Fort Leavenworth, Kans., to Sheridan, Aug. 6, 1880, *ibid.;* see also Santa Fe *Weekly New Mexican,* Aug. 16, 1880.

[51] Sheridan to AG, Chicago, Aug. 15, 1880, *ibid.;* see also Santa Fe *Weekly New Mexican,* Aug. 14, 16, 23, 1880.

CHAPTER VII

[1] Hatch to AAG, Fort Leavenworth, Kans., Sept. 10, 1880, *Victorio File.*

[2] Ord to AG, San Antonio, Aug. 25, 1880, *ibid.*

[3] Gillett, *Six Years with the Texas Rangers,* 184–87; Webb, *Texas Rangers,* 401; more information on the Rangers in this Victorio campaign can be found in Carlysle Graham Raht, *The Romance of Davis Mountains and Big Bend Country* (El Paso: RAHTbooks, 1919).

[4] J. C. Tiffany to Commissioner of Indian Affairs, San Carlos Agency, July 20, 1880, *Victorio File.*

[5] Ord to AG, San Antonio, Aug. 27, 1880, *ibid.*

[6] Pope to AG, Chicago, Sept. 10, 1880, *ibid.*

[7] J. Fred Rippy, "Some Precedents of the Pershing Expedition into Mexico," *Southwestern Historical Quarterly,* XXIV (April 1921), 292–316.

[8] See *Diplomatic Despatches.*

[9] *New York Times,* Aug. 10, 1880; see also *San Antonio Express,* Aug. 18, 25, 1880.

[10] See King, *War Eagle,* 192; doubtless, this Mexican leader was Leonardo Márquez, although King and others do not reveal his complete name.

[11] *San Antonio Express,* Aug. 22, 1880.

[12] Russell to Commissioner of Indian Affairs, Mescalero Agency, Sept. 6, 1880, *Victorio File.*

[13] Boston, *Daily Advertiser,* Oct. 12, 1880, *ibid.*

[14] Colonel George Buell to AAG, Oct. 22, 1880, ibid.; see also Martin L. Crimmons, "Colonel Buell's Expedition into Mexico in 1880," *New Mexico Historical Review,* X (April 1935), 133–42.

[15] Gillett, *Six Years with the Rangers,* p. 184.

[16] For more information see Terrazas, *Memorias.*

[17] Mexicans knew well how serious border conditions were, and still they feared United States troops on their soil. Specifically, see Francisco Almada, *Resumen de Historia Del Estado de Chihuahua* (Mexico, D.F.: Libros Mexicos, 1955); see also the very valuable work, Daniel Cosío Villegas (ed.), *Historia Moderna De Mexico,* 7 vols. (Mexico, D.F.: Editorial Hermes, 1955–65). The Terrazas regime is discussed in Robert Sandels, "Silvestre Terrazas and the Old Regime in Chihuahua," *Americas,* 28 (Oct. 1971), 191–205.

[18] Sheridan to AG, Chicago, Oct. 22, 1880, *Victorio File.*

[19] Gillett, *Six Years with the Texas Rangers,* pp. 185–87.

[20] Buell to AAG, El Paso, Oct. 15, 1880, *Victorio File.*

[21] Jordán, *Crónica de un Pais Bárbaro;* see also Terrazas, *Memorias.*

[22] Buell to AAG, Santa Fe, Oct. 22, 1880, *Victorio File;* see also *San Antonio Express,* Oct. 22, 23, 1880; Santa Fe *Weekly New Mexican,* Dec. 6, 1880.

[23] William Evarts to Alexander Ramsey, Washington, D.C., Nov. 8, 1880, *ibid.*

[24] Ord to AG, San Antonio, Oct. 30, 1880, *ibid.;* a reminiscence of this event, perhaps mixed with information acquired after the battle, can be found in Ball, *In the Days of Victorio.*

[25] Santa Fe *Weekly New Mexican*, Oct. 25, 1880.

[26] Chávez, "Extinción de los Apaches," 346.

[27] Santa Fe *Weekly New Mexican,* Dec. 6, 1880; see story of Victorio's death in Cimarron *News and Press,* Oct. 28, 1880.

[28] Hermosillo, *La Constitución,* Nov. 18, 1880; James Kaywaykla, *In the Days of Victorio,* claimed Victorio killed himself after a fierce fight. There are so many different stories concerning Victorio's origins, his leadership, and his death that it is impossible to ascertain precisely what occurred. Moreover, although Army reports appear fairly complete, they too must be read and relied upon cautiously.

BIBLIOGRAPHY

GOVERNMENT DOCUMENTS

Bigelow, Major John, Jr. *Tenth United States Cavalry, Historical Sketch, 1866–92.* Found in RG 98 Records of United States Army Commands.

Crooke, George, *Resumé of Operations Against Apache Indians, 1882–1886.* Washington, D.C., Government Printing Office, 1887.

Heitman, Francis B. *Historical Register and Dictionary of the United States Army From Its Organization, September 29, 1789, to March 2, 1903.* 2 vols. Urbana, University of Illinois Press, 1965.

United States Government. National Archives and Record Service. Letters Received, Selected Documents Relating to the Activities of the Ninth and Tenth Cavalry in the Campaign Against Victorio, 1879–1880. File 6058-1879, Record Group 94.

Records of Engagements with Hostile Indians within the Military Division of the Missouri, from 1868 to 1822, compiled from official records. Washington, D.C., Government Printing Office, 1882.

Records of the Office of Indian Affairs, New Mexico superintendency.

Records of the War Department, Adjutant General's Office, Record Group 94, various post returns and letters received.

United States Congress, *House Exec. Doc.,* No. 1, Part 2, 45 Cong., 3 sess.

United States Congress, *House Exec. Doc.* 50, 30 Cong., 2 sess., Ser. 541.

United States Department of the Interior, Territorial Papers, New Mexico, 1851–1914, Executive Proceedings, October 8, 1774–December 31, 1881; see also *Report of the Commissioner of Indian Affairs.*

United States Department of State, Despatches from U. S. Ministers to Mexico, 1823–1906, Record Group 59, National Archives. Microfilm copy, Oklahoma State University Library.

United States Department of War. *Annual Report of the Secretary of War for the Years 1866–1891.*

The War of the Rebellion: A Compilation of the Official Records of the Union and Confederate Armies. 128 vols. Washington, D.C., Government Printing Office, 1880–1901.

PRIMARY SOURCES

Ball, Eve. *In the Days of Victorio: Recollections of a Warm Springs Apache, James Kaywaykla Narrator.* Tucson: University of Arizona Press, 1970.

Baylor, George W. *John Robert Baylor: Confederate Governor of Arizona.* Ed. by Odie B. Faulk. Tucson: Arizona Historical Society, 1966.

Bourke, John G. *On the Border with Crook.* New York: Scribners, 1891, and reprints.

Clum, John P. "Apache Misrule," *New Mexico Historical Review,* V (April, July 1930), pp. 138–53; 221–39.

———. "The Apaches," *New Mexico Historical Review,* IV (April 1929), pp. 107–27.

———. "Geronimo," *New Mexico Historical Review,* III (Jan., April, July 1928), pp. 1–40; 121–44; 217–64.

———. "Victorio," *Arizona Historical Review,* II (Jan. 1930), pp. 74–90.

Cruse, Thomas. *Apache Days and After,* 70–77. Caldwell, Ida.: Caxton Press, 1941. These pages deal with Hatch and Victorio when the latter encamped at Hembrillo Canyon.

Flipper, Henry Ossian, *The Colored Cadet at West Point.* New York: H. Lee, 1878.

Gatewood, Charles B. "Campaigning Against Victorio in 1879," *The Great Divide* (April 1894), pp. 102–4.

Gillett, James B. *Six Years with the Texas Rangers.* New Haven: Yale University Press, 1925, reprinted 1963, pp. 183–89.

———. *The Texas Ranger: A Story of the Southwestern Frontier.* Chicago: World Book Co., 1927.

Howard, Oliver O. *My Life and Experience Among Our Hostile Indians.* Hartford: N. D. Worthington, 1907.

Terrazas, D. Joaquin. *Memorias.* Imprenta de "El Agricultor Mexicano" Juarez: Escobar Hnos., 1905.

Wallace, Lew. *An Autobiography.* 2 vols. New York, Somerset, 1906.

NEWSPAPERS

Boston *Daily Advertiser.*
Cimarron *The News and Press.*
Hermosillo (Sonora) *La Constitución.*
Las Cruces *Thirty-Four.*
New York Times.
San Antonio Express.
Santa Fe *Weekly New Mexican.*
Silver City *Daily Southwest.*
Silver City *Grant County Herald.*
Silver City *Herald.*
Socorro Sun.
St. Louis *Republican.*

SECONDARY SOURCES

Almada, Francisco R. *Resumen de Historia del Estado de Chihuahua.* Mexico, D.F.: Libros Mexicanos, 1955.

Asburn, P. M. *A History of the Medical Department of the United States Army.* Boston: Houghton Mifflin, 1929.

Ball, Eve. "The Apache Scouts, A Chiricahua Appraisal," *Arizona and the West* (Winter, 1965), 315–28.

Brandes, Ray. "Don Santiago Kirker, King of the Scalp Hunters," *The Smoke Signal,* (Fall 1962), 2–8.

Bancroft, Hubert H. *History of Arizona and New Mexico,* XVII. San Francisco: History Co., 1889.

————. *History of the North Mexican States and Texas.* 2 vols. San Francisco: History Co., 1884–1889.

Brandes, Ray. *Frontier Military Posts of Arizona.* Globe, Ariz.: Dale Stuart King, Publisher, 1960.

Basso, Keith H. (ed.). *Western Apache Raiding and Warfare: From the Notes of Grenville Goodwin.* Tucson: University of Arizona Press, 1971.

Beck, Warren A. *New Mexico: A History of Four Centuries.* Norman: University of Oklahoma Press, 1962.

Brinkerhoff, Sidney B., and Odie B. Faulk. *Lancers for the King.* Phoenix: Arizona Historical Foundation, 1965.

Chávez, José Carlos. "El indio 'Victorio,' " *Boletín de la Sociedad Chihuahuense de Estudios Historicos,* V (Aug. 1944), 509–13.

————. "Extinción de los Apaches," *Boletín de la Sociedad Chihuahuense de Estudios Históricos,* I (April 1939), 336–77.

Conner, Daniel Ellis. *Joseph Reddeford Walker and the Arizona Adventure.* Ed. by Donald J. Berthrong and Odessa Davenport. Norman: University of Oklahoma Press, 1956.

Crimmons, Martin L. "Colonel Buell's Expedition into Mexico in 1880," *New Mexico Historical Review,* 10 (1935), 133–42.

Diccionario Porrua Historia, Biografía y Geografía de Mexico. 2nd Mexico, D. F.: Editorial Porrua, 1964.

Dinges, Bruce J. "The Court-Martial of Lieutenant Henry O. Flipper: An Example of Black-White Relations in the Army," *American West,* IX (Jan. 1972), 12–61.

Downey, Fairfax. *Indian-fighting Army.* New York: Scribner's, 1941.

————. *Indian Wars of the U.S. Army 1776–1865.* New York: Doubleday, 1963.

Forbes, Jack D. *Apache, Navajo, and Spaniard.* Norman: University of Oklahoma Press, 1960.

Foreman, Grant. *Fort Gibson: A Brief History.* Norman: University of Oklahoma Press, 1943.

Fulton, Maurice Garland. *History of the Lincoln County War.* Ed. by Robert N. Mullin. Tucson: University of Arizona Press, 1968.

Glass, Major E. L. N. (comp. and ed.). *The History of the Tenth Cavalry, 1866–1921.* Tucson: Acme Printing Co., 1921.

Gregg, Andy. *Drums of Yesterday: The Forts of New Mexico.* Santa Fe: Press of the Territorian, 1968.

Haley, J. Evetts. *Fort Concho and the Texas Frontier.* San Angelo, Tex.: San Angelo Standard Times, 1952.

Hamill, Hugh M. *The Hidalgo Revolt: Prelude to Mexican Independence.* Gainesville: University of Florida Press, 1966.

Hastings, James R. "The Tragedy of Camp Grant in 1871," *Arizona and the West,* XI, 2 (Summer 1959), 146–60.

Heard, J. Norman. *The Black Frontiersman: Adventures of Negroes Among American Indians 1528–1918.* New York, John Day, 1969.

Hutchins, James S. "Mounted Riflemen: The Real Role of Cavalry in the Indian Wars," *El Palacio,* 69 (Summer 1962), 85–91.

Jordán, Fernando. *Crónica de Un País Bárbaro.* 2nd ed. Mexico: Talleres de B. Costa-Amic, 1965.

Keleher, William A. *Turmoil in New Mexico, 1846–1868.* Santa Fe: Rydal Press, 1952.

———. *Violence in Lincoln County, 1869–1881.* Albuquerque: University of New Mexico Press, 1967.

Kenner, Charles L. *A History of New-Mexican–Plains-Indian Relations.* Norman: University of Oklahoma Press, 1969.

King, James T. *War Eagle: A Life of General Eugene A. Carr.* Lincoln: University of Nebraska Press, 1963.

Kropp, Simon. "Albert J. Fountain and the Fight for Public Education in New Mexico," *Arizona and the West,* XI (Winter 1969), 341–58.

Leckie, William H. *The Buffalo Soldiers: A Narrative of the Negro Cavalry in the West.* Norman: University of Oklahoma Press, 1967.

Lockwood, Frank C. *The Apache Indians.* New York: Macmillan, 1938.

Mayne, Reid. *The Scalp Hunters: A Romance of Northern Mexico.* London: Seeley and Co., n.d.

Moorhead, Max L. *The Apache Frontier: Jacobo Ugarte and Spanish–Indian Relations in Northern New Spain, 1769–1791.* Norman: University of Oklahoma Press, 1968.

Nye, Wilbur S. *Carbine & Lance: The Story of Old Fort Sill.* Norman: University of Oklahoma Press, 1969.

Ochoa, Humberto E. *Integración y Desintegración de Nuestra Frontera Norte.* Mexico: Universidad Nacional, 1949.

Ogle, Ralph H. *Federal Control of the Western Apaches: 1848–1886.* Albuquerque: University of New Mexico Press, 1940.

Quarles, Benjamin. *The Negro in the Civil War.* Boston: Little, Brown, 1953.

Raht, Carlysle G. *The Romance of Davis Mountains and Big Bend Country.* El Paso: RAHTbooks Co., 1919.

Reeve, Frank D. "The Federal Indian Policy in New Mexico, 1858–1880," *New Mexico Historical Review,* XII (July, 1937), 218–69; XIII (Jan., April, July 1938), 14–62, 146–91, 261–313.

Roeder, Ralph. *Juárez and His Mexico.* 2 vols. New York: Viking, 1947.

Reddick, L. D. "The Negro Policy of the United States Army," *Journal of Negro History,* XXIV (Jan. 1949), 14–15.

Rickey, Don, Jr. *Forty Miles a Day on Beans and Hay: The Enlisted Soldier Fighting the Indian Wars.* Norman: University of Oklahoma Press, 1963.

Rippy, J. Fred. "Some Precedents of the Pershing Expedition into Mexico," *Southwestern Historical Quarterly,* XXIV (April 1921), 292–316.

Romero, Manuel. "Victor el Apache que creo mi madre era hijo del gran jefe de los Apaches 'Victorio,' " *Boletín de la Sociedad Chihuahuense de Estudios Históricos,* VI (Jan.–Feb. 1944), 509–13.

Ross, Stanley R. *Francisco I. Madero, Apostle of Mexican Democracy.* New York: Columbia University Press, 1955.

Sandels, Robert. "Silvestre Terrazas and the Old Regime in Chihuahua," *Americas,* 28 (Oct. 1971), 191–205.

Seymour, Flora W. *Indian Agents of the Old Frontier.* New York: Appleton-Century-Crofts, 1941.

Sacks, B. "New Evidence on the Bascom Affair," *Arizona and the West,* IV (Autumn 1962), 261–78.

Smith, Ralph A. "Apache Plunder Trails Southward, 1831–1840," *New Mexico Historical Review,* XXXVII (Jan. 1962), 20–42.

———. "Apache 'Ranching' Below the Gila, 1841–1845," *Arizonian,* III (Winter 1962), 1–17.

———. "John Joel Glanton, Lord of the Scalp Range," *Smoke Signal,* VI (Fall 1962), 9–16.

———. "The Scalp Hunt in Chihuahua—1849," *New Mexico Historical Review,* XL (April 1965), 116–40.

———. "The Scalp Hunter in the Borderlands, 1835–1850," *Arizona and the West,* VI (Spring 1964), 5–22.

Spicer, Edward H. *Cycles of Conquest: The Impact of Spain, Mexico, and the United States on the Indians of the Southwest.* Tucson: University of Arizona Press, 1962.

Stout, Joseph A., Jr. *The Liberators: Filibustering Expeditions into Mexico, 1848–1862 and the Last Thrust of Manifest Destiny.* Los Angeles: Westernlore Press, 1973.

Tatum, Lawrie. *Our Red Brothers and the Peace Policy of President Ulysses S. Grant.* Lincoln: University of Nebraska Press, 1971.

Temple, Frank M. "Colonel Grierson in the Southwest," *Panhandle Plains Historical Review,* 30 (1957), 27–54.

———. "Colonel B. H. Grierson's Victorio Campaign," *West Texas Historical Association Year Book,* XXXV (Oct. 1959), 99–111.

Thompson, Erwin N. "The Negro Soldiers on the Frontier: A Fort Davis Case Study," *Journal of the West,* VII (April 1968), 217–35.

Thrapp, Dan L. *The Conquest of Apacheria.* Norman: University of Oklahoma Press, 1967.

Turner, John K. *Barbarous Mexico.* Austin: University of Texas Press, 1969.

Tyler, Barbara. "Cochise: Apache War Leader," *Journal of Arizona History,* VI (Spring 1965), 1–10.

Utley, Robert M. *Fort Davis National Historic Site, Texas.* Washington, D.C.: National Park Service Historical Handbook, Series No. 38, 1965.

———. "The Bascom Affair: A Reconstruction," *Arizona and the West,* III (Spring 1961), 59–68.

Villegas, Daniel Cosío. (ed). *Historia Moderna de Mexico.* 7 vols. Mexico, D. F.: Editorial Hermes, 1955–65.

Wagoner, Jay J. *Arizona Territory, 1863–1912: A Political History.* Tucson: University of Arizona Press, 1970.

Webb, Walter P. *The Texas Rangers: A Century of Frontier Defense.* Boston: Houghton-Mifflin, 1935.

Wharfield, Colonel H. B. *10th Cavalry and Border Fights.* El Cajon, Calif.: privately printed, 1965.

Woodward, Arthur H. "Side Lights on Fifty Years of Apache Warfare 1936–1886," *Arizoniana,* II (Fall 1961), 3–14.

Wormser, Richard. *The Yellowlegs: The Story of the United States Cavalry.* New York: Doubleday, 1966.

INDEX

Aleman's Well (N.M.), 129, 132; Army rests at, 124

Albuquerque (N.M.), 87

Almonte, Juan N., colonization plan of, 10-11

Amaya, Don Simón, 147

Animas Canyon (N.M.), 98

Apaches, 11, 12, 13, 14, 15, 22, 31, 39, 41; heritage and culture, 3-6; ally with Spaniards against Comanches, 6; use modern weapons, 8; hunted for scalps, 11-14; failure of intruders to understand, 19-20; attitude toward white concepts of boundaries, 21; government policy toward, 23; harass troops at forts in Arizona, 27; Union and Confederate attitudes toward during Civil War, 27-30; Tucsonians attack, 32-33; Crook's method of tracking, 34; at San Carlos with Clum, 35-36; pressured to live on reservations in New Mexico, 37; effect of Lincoln County War on, 44-47; removed to San Carlos, 47-50; at San Carlos, picture of, 48; Gatewood's attitudes toward, 79; natural animosity of factions toward each other, 89; as captives at Fort Bowie, picture of, 95; ability to vanish into mountains, 101; at Battle of Carrizal, 116-17; Pope's attitude toward, 118-19; disarmed at Tularosa, 136; in Battle of Eagle Springs, 153

Aranda, Don Ramón, 171; Texas Rangers visit, 116

Aravaipa Apaches, as victims at Camp Grant, 32-33

Arispe (Sonora), threatened by Indians, 7

Arista, Mariano, President of Mexico, 16

Arizona: Indian raids in, 7; becomes military district, 30-31; becomes separate Department, 32

Army, United States: description of, during Indian Wars, 51-74; structure, organization, discipline, 51-74; health difficulties, 57; strength of elements chasing Victorio, 111; seeks solution to prob-

Army, United States (*continued*)
lem of Ojo Calientes, 134-57; final
campaign against Ojo Calientes,
158-79
Ash Creek (N.M.), 81
Ashenfelter, S. M., 42, 150
Athapascans, linguistic group, 4
Augur, General C. C., commands
Department of Texas, 71
Axtell, Samuel, Governor of New
Mexico, 45, 46, 104

Bascom, George N., 24-27
"Bascom Affair," 24-27
Baylor, George W.: leader of Texas
Rangers, 113-14, 116, 125, 159,
160, 163, 170, 171, 174, 175;
picture of, 114
Baylor, John R.: Governor of Con-
federate Territory of Arizona, 27,
29; picture of, 29
Bazaine, Marshal Francisco A.,
leads French troops in Mexico, 17
Ben Hur (novel by Lew Wallace), 46
Bennett, F. T., 85, 86
Berger, Charles, Indian scout, 170
Beyer, Charles D., 96-97, 121, 143,
169, 170; chases Apaches, 88
Beyer's Ranch, 169
Big Bend country (Texas), Army
chases Apaches into, 90
Black cavalrymen ("buffalo sol-
diers"), 51-74; praised by news-
paper, 128, 142
Black soldiers, picture of, at Fort
Bayard, 53
Blocksom, Augustus P., 96, 97,
100, 102; searches for Apaches,
94
Board of Indian Commissioners, 31
Bocco Grande Pass (Mexico), 169
Bonney, William (Billy the Kid), 45,
46, 180

Borracho (Mexico), 174; Buell at,
171
Bosque Redondo, 37; reservation
constructed, 30
Buell, George P., 171, 175; enters
Mexico, 170; ordered out of Mexico, 171
"Buffalo soldiers," *see* Black cavalrymen
Bureau of Indian Affairs, 31, 35, 79,
85, 87, 181
Byrne, James J., 174; killed by Indians, 158

Calhoun, James S., Superintendent
of Indian Affairs for New Mex-
ico, 22, 23
California, state sends troops to
punish Yumas, 15
California Column, 29
Calvo, José J., Governor of
Chihuahua, 12
Camp Grant (Ariz.), 32, 40; attack,
37
Camp Grant Massacre, 33
Camp Huachuca (Ariz.), 94
Camp Verde (Ariz.), 35
Camp Wichita, Tenth Cavalry or-
dered to, 68
Cañada Alamosa (N.M.), 40, 41, 43,
44; Ojo Calientes settle near, 39,
40
Cañada del Marranas River (Mex-
ico), 116
Canada, Sioux flee to, 75
Canby, E. R. S.: picture of, 26;
commands Union troops in New
Mexico, 27
Candalaría Mountains, 112, 159,
161, 170, 172, 175
Carasco, José M., military Governor
of Sonora, 8, 9
Carleton, James H., commands
California Column, 29, 30, 37

Carpenter, L. H., 157
Carr, Eugene A., 119, 170, 180; searches for Apaches, 94; picture of, 120; critizes Hatch, 151; blocks Márquez, 167
Carralitos (Mexico), 147
Carrizal (Mexico), 147, 173, 178; Mexicans massacred at, 116
Carrizos Mountains (Chihuahua), 157
Carroll, Henry, 122, 129, 130, 131; picture of, 123
Casavantes, Jesus José, heads revolutionary forces, 19
Castellanos, Victor, 177
Chávez, Cesaria, 177
Chávez, José C., 147
Chiricahua Apaches, 24, 29, 44, 76, 78; willingness to fight whites, 23, 27; remain free after Crook's efforts, 34; agree to settle on a reservation, 35
Chiricahua Reservation (Ariz.), 43
Chisum, John, in Lincoln County War, 45
Cisheros, Ponciano, 173
Civil War, 27; effect of end on New Mexico, 30
Clum, John P.: agent at San Carlos, 35-36, 47, 48, 49, 50; picture of, 36; and Apaches at Washington, picture of, 49; and Apache police, 48-50; resigns, 50; receives orders to remove Ojo Calientes to San Carlos, 78
Cochise, Apache chief, 27, 41; attitude toward Mexicans and Americans, 24; reasons for attitude toward Americans, 24-26; picture of, 25; agrees to treaty, 35; dies, 43
Colorado River, scalp hunters at, 14
Columbus, original voyage noted, 20
Columbus Barracks (Ohio), 55

Colyer, Vincent: heads peace commission, 33; leaves Arizona, 34
Comanche Indians: fight Apache-Spanish alliance, 6, 7; scalp hunters harass, 12-13; Texas Rangers fight, 27; Tenth Cavalry fights, 73; renegades with Victorio, 131
Conde, Francisco García, Governor of Chihuahua, 12
Confederate invasion of New Mexico, 27
Conline, John, 129, 130
Cook's Canyon, (N.M.), 152; Morrow catches Apaches at, 145
Cooney, Jim, Indians attack camp of, 137
Cordero, José, Governor of Chihuahua, 16
Corral de Piedras (Mexico), 171
Corredor, Mauricio el, kills Victorio, 176, 179
Corruption, as factor in Indian problems, 47, 181
Cota, Jesus, 174; ranch attacked, 159
Crawford, Jack, Indian scout, 170
Crook, George, commands Army in Arizona, 34-35
Crouch, O., 101
Crow Springs (Texas), Indians attack, 125
Cruse, Thomas, 131
Cuchillo Negro, Apache chief, 76
Cuchillo Negro (N.M.), 39, 129
Custer, George A., 54

Dalrymple, Ernest, filibuster, 166-67
David's Island (N.Y.), 55
Davidson, John W., 68
Dawson, Byron, 121; chases Victorio, 94, 96; men trapped, 96
Day, M. W., decorated for bravery, 97
Del Alamo (N.M.), 155

Diablo, Apache policeman, picture of, 36
Díaz, Porfirio, 146, 163, 164, 168; begins revolution, 18; controls Mexico, 104
District of the Pecos, 73
Dog Canyon (N.M.), Army and Indians fight in, 136
Donovan County (N.M.), 102
Drew, Charles E., agent of southern New Mexico, 39
Dudley, L. E., Indian Superintendent, 41, 90
Durango (Mexico), Indians ravage, 13

Eagle Springs Mountains (Texas), 66, 152, 153, 154, 159
El Chaparro (Mexico), 174
El Cobre Mountains, 172
El Lucero (Mexico), Buell near, 170
El Paso (Texas), 27, 66, 73, 104, 113, 114, 148, 150, 155, 158, 169
Elías, Jesus M., leads citizens in Camp Grant Massacre, 33
Elkins, Stephen B., 58
Escalante y Arvizu, Leonardo, Governor of Sonora, 11
Eskiminzin, Apache policeman, picture of, 32, 36

Felix (Mickey Free), Indian scout, 24
Filibustering, as threat to Mexico, 166-68
Finley, Leighton, 153, 154
Flipper, Henry O., 51, 63, 154-55
Florida Mountains (N.M.), 118, 121
Fort Apache (Ariz.), 86
Fort Bayard (N.M.), 37, 39, 94, 96, 97, 108, 118; gatehouse, picture of, 98; barracks building, picture of, 97; officer's quarters, picture of, 108; picture of, 109

Fort Bowie (Ariz.), 29, 94; picture of, 95
Fort Breckenridge (Ariz.), 27
Fort Buchanan (Ariz.), 24, 27
Fort Concho (Texas), 61, 69, 73, 88, 119, 134, 135
Fort Craig (N.M.), 140
Fort Cummings (N.M.), 88, 97, 145, 146, 159, 162
Fort Davis (Texas), 65, 66, 67, 68, 73, 89, 101, 134, 148, 152, 154; barracks and corrals, picture of, 64; commanding officer's quarters, picture of, 65; officers' row, picture of, 166
Fort Gibson (Indian Territory), 67
Fort Grant (Ariz.), 14, 119
Fort Lowell (Ariz.), 94
Fort McKavett (Texas), 69
Fort Quitman (N.M.), 69, 153, 154, 155, 157, 158, 161, 162, 171
Fort San Carlos (Ariz.), picture of, 42
Fort Selden (N.M.), 37
Fort Sill (Indian Territory), 64; picture of, 67
Fort Stanton Reservation (N.M.), 91, 107, 122, 129, 150; Indians raid from, 89
Fort Stockton (Texas), 65, 68, 71, 119
Fort Wingate (N.M.), 81, 127
Fort Worth (Texas), 27
Fountain, Albert J., organizes militia, 142
France, intervenes in Mexico, 17-18
French, J. Hansel, killed, 121
Fresco River (N.M.), Army rests at, 139

Galeana (Chihuahua), scalp hunters attack, 13
Gatewood, Charles B., 94, 96, 97, 98, 99, 100, 105, 118, 130, 135,

136, 148; as leader of Indian scouts, 79; picture of, 80

Geronimo, Apache war chief, 47, 102, 139, 175

Gila River, scalp hunting near, 12

Gillett, James B.: Texas Ranger, 114, 116, 125, 126, 158, 172, 174; picture of, 115

Gilmore, John C.: warns of Victorio's approach, 153; escorts wagon train, 156

Glanton, John J., scalp hunter, 14-15

Godfroy, Frederick C., Indian agent, 86

Gordo, Captain, joins Terrazas, 147

Grant County (N.M.), citizens condemn Hatch, 143

Grant, U. S.: peace policy of, 31, 33, 39; approves Tularosa Reservation, 41; endorses Hatch, 61

Greiner, John, 23

Grierson, Benjamin H., 61, 63, 64, 67, 68, 73, 134-35, 146, 147, 148, 152, 153, 154, 155, 157, 160, 161, 177, 180; picture of, 62

Grierson, Robert (son of Benjamin), 153

Gross, Sergeant, killed, 121

Guadalupe Hidalgo, Treaty of, 13-14, 21-22

Guadalupe (Mexico), Texas Rangers at, 116

Guadalupe Mountains (Texas), 119, 124, 136, 155

Guerrero (Mexico), 147, 174

Guzman's Springs (Mexico), 170

Hacienda del Carmen (Mexico), 173

Halcon Negro, Apache chief, 75

Hart, H. L., succeeds Clum, 50, 78

Hatch, Edward, 43, 44, 47, 60, 61, 69, 71, 74, 84, 86, 88, 91, 100, 101, 104, 105, 118, 119, 121, 122, 123, 124, 126, 128, 131, 132, 135, 137, 138, 139, 140, 141, 142, 143, 144, 146, 148, 149, 150, 151, 152, 153; picture of, 60; ignores courier from Parker, 140; defends actions, 141

Hayes, Rutherford B., 139

Hembrillo Canyon (N.M.), Victorio at, 128, 129, 130

Hennisee, A. G., Indian agent, 40

Herrera, José Joaquín de: colonization law of, 9; President of Mexico, 16

Hidalgo y Castillo, Miguel, declares Mexican independence, 6

Hillsboro (N.M.), 92, 96

Hooker, Ambrose E., 92, 94, 101, 105, 106, 122

Howard, Guy, searches for Apaches, 94

Howard, Oliver Otis, leads peace commission, 34-35, 41

Hunkpapa Sioux, 75

Indian Bureau, dishonesty in, 15

James, F. W., 167

Janos (Chihuahua), 8

Jefferson Barracks (Mo.), 55

Jeffords, Thomas J., 35

Johnson, James, scalp hunter, 11

Jones, Thaddeus W., 156

Jones, W. T., 102

Juárez, Benito, fights France, 17, 18

Juárez (Mexico), 113, 147

Juh, Apache leader, 139

Kaywaykla, James, survivor of Victorio's band, 177-78

Kemble, E. C., 43, 44

Kickapoo Indians, raid frontier, 68

Killdegoing, ———, Indians kill, 139

Kirker, James, scalp hunter, 11-15

La Quadria (Mexico), Texas Rangers near, 116
Lafaya, Luis, 135
Laguna Palomas (Chihuahua), 146
Lardizabal, captured by Apaches, 76
Las Animas River (N.M.), 96
Las Cruces (N.M.), 121; citizens angry about Indian attacks, 91, 92; volunteers from, 102
Las Lagunas (Mexico), 173
Lawlessness, as contributing factor in Indian Wars, 44-47
Lebo, Thomas C., 157
Lerdist party, members occupy Paso del Norte, 18
Ley Quinto, scalp bounty law, 14
Limpia Canyon, Indians raid ranch at, 89
Limpia Creek, location of Fort Davis, 65
Little Big Horn, Battle of, 75
Lincoln County War, 39, 44-47, 180, 183
Lipan Apaches, with Victorio, 91
Livermore, William R., 160
Llanas de las Castillas (Mexico), 176
Loco, chief of Apaches, 39, 41; picture of, 39
Long, Jack, 100

Madden, Dan, 138, 151, 159; leads volunteers, 137
Madden, Emery S., killed, 159
Malpi Station (N.M.), picture of, 43
Maney, James, 121, 169, 171, 174
Mangas Coloradas: insight into attitude toward Americans, 23-24, 27; captured and killed, 29-30, 76
Mariano, leader of Navajo scouts, 122
Márquez, Leonardo, Mexican revolutionary, 167-68
Martin's Well (N.M.), 123

Maximilian, Emperor of Mexico, 17
Mazatlán (Sonora), Apaches attack near, 16
McCrary, William W., Secretary of War, 92
McEvers Ranch, 102, 105; Indians attack, 92
McLellan, Curwen B., 119, 129, 130, 131
McSween, Alexander, in Lincoln County War, 45, 46
Merritt, Wesley, 69, 87; picture of, at West Point, 52; picture of, as general and commander at Fort Davis, 70
Mescalero Apaches, 40, 68, 73, 76, 132, 135, 137, 144, 148, 149, 157; willingness to fight whites, 23; quartered at Bosque Redondo, 30, 37; with Victorio, 91, 107, 131, 134; Hatch's attitude toward, 126; effect of disarming on Victorio, 151
Mesilla (N.M.), 27, 29; volunteers from, 102
Mesilla Valley, 37; citizens organize defenses at, 142
Mexican Chamber of Deputies, colonization plans considered by, 10
Mexican War, 8, 9
Mexicans, massacred at Carrizal, 112
Mexico: independence of, 6-7; instability of, 7; frontier conditions worsen, 8-9; colonization efforts, 9-11; liberal-conservative struggle, 16-18; attempts to resolve Indian problems, 20; internal difficulties, 103
Mills, Anson, 119
Mimbres Apaches: reasons for hating whites, 11; Mangas Coloradas as a member of, 24; John Baylor's

plans against, 29; Victorio's background with, 76

Mimbres Mountains (N.M.), 3, 96, 101, 107, 119, 121

Mogollon Mountains, (N.M.), 101, 119; Victorio in Black Range, 90, 107, 132; Black Range mentioned, 137

Morrow, Albert P., 69, 74, 87, 88, 94, 96, 100, 101, 102, 105, 106, 107, 108, 111, 112, 118, 121, 122, 123, 124, 136, 137, 139, 145, 152; joins Black units, 63

Murphy, Lawrence G., in Lincoln County War, 45, 46

Nana, Apache chief, 94, 132, 178; picture of, 93

Natanes Mountains, Victorio's band in, 81

Navajo Indians, 23, 30, 37, 122, 145; as scouts, 94, 96; scouts suffer losses, 98; scout killed, 123

New Mexico: raids in, 7; Department of, 37; Territory, map of, 82-83

Newport Barracks (Ky.), 55

Nolan, Nicholas, arrives to fight Apaches, 154, 155

Northern Mexico, map of, 164-65

Ochoa, Antonio, 18

Ojo Caliente Apaches: economy and political-social system of, 4; refuse to remain on reservation, 15, 44; settle near Cañada Alamosa, 39; seek own reservation, 39-42; moved to Ojo Caliente reservation, 41; prepare to fight against removal to San Carlos, 43; first outbreak of, 75-110; pursued by civilians, Rangers, and Mexicans, 111-33; final months of freedom, 158-79

Ojo Caliente Reservation, 44, 47, 49, 84, 87, 90, 110, 122, 126, 127, 155

Ojo del Pino (Mexico), 153

Ord, E. O. C., 87, 161-63; replaces Augur, 71, 73; picture of, 72

Ortiz, Juan Mata, 176

Oury, William S., leads citizens in Camp Grant Massacre, 33

Padilla, Pirso, 177

Palomas (N.M.), Apaches near, 122

Palomas River, 140, 144, 169

Panic of 1873, 55

Papago Indians, 35; in Camp Grant Massacre, 33

Paredes, Mariano, colonization plan of, 10

Parker, Ely, Commissioner of Indian Affairs, 31

Parker, H. K., 144; continues chasing Victorio, 139-40

Parker, James, 174

Patrillo Mountains (Mexico), 69

Pecos River, 30, 150

Pile, William A., Governor of New Mexico, 40

Pima Indians, 35

Pine Mountains (Mexico), 170

Pionsenay, Apache renegade, 78, 79

Piper, Orland F., Indian agent, 40–41

Plan de Ayutla, favors federalist constitution, 16

Plan de la Noria, 146

Plan of Tuxtepec, 146

Pope, John, 92, 100, 102, 107, 117, 118, 126, 162; defends Hatch, 149-50; travels to New Mexico, 150

Pope, Nathaniel, Indian Superintendent, 40

Porfiristas, 18, 19

Presbyterian Board of Foreign Missions, 40
Purington, George A., 121

"Quaker Policy," 31
Quitman Canyon, Battle of, 154–55

Ranchería Mountains (Mexico), 172
Rattlesnake Springs (Texas), 157, 160; Grierson at, 155
Rebosadero Springs (Mexico), 174
Rio Cuchillo Negro, 106
Rio Grande, 68, 74, 122, 137, 140, 152, 153, 157, 170
Rio Marcos, 150
Rio Percha (N.M.), 90
Rio Puerco (N.M.), 121
Ritch, William G., Acting Governor of New Mexico, 126-27, 135
Robrs, Isaac, killed, 159
Romero, Manuel, 75
Royal Regulations of 1772, 6
Rubí, Marques de, administrative reforms of, 6
Rucker, Louis, 122, 124
Russell, S. A.: agent, 91, 134, 136, 137, 149, 151; appointed agent at Tularosa, 87; complains about Army's actions, 148; reports depredations, 168–69
Rynerson, W. L., in Lincoln County War, 39

Sacramento Mountains (N.M.), 132, 136
Safford, A. P. K., Governor of Arizona, 33
St. Louis (Mo.), Grierson sent to, 68
Samaniego, Don Mariano, 178; ranch raided, 171
San Andres (Mexico), 173, 174; Terrazas nears, 147

San Andres Mountains (N.M.), 90, 124, 129, 137
San Antonio (Texas), 66, 73, 161; picture of, 112, 113; Baylor at, 113
San Carlos Reservation (Ariz.), 34, 42, 43, 47, 48, 49, 50, 78, 79, 80, 85, 86, 87, 90, 94, 102, 126, 127, 137, 139, 141, 146, 161
San Fernando de Taos, scalp hunters attack, 12
San José (Mexico), 129, 172
San Lorenzo, 146, 153
San Mateo Mountains, 88, 107, 121, 137
San Pedro River, 27
San Saba River, 69
Santa Anna, Antonio López de, 16
Santa Barbara (N.M.), Indians attack, 102
Santa Fe (N.M.), 124, 126; Clum at, 35; picture of, 105; and traders, picture of, 106; Dalrymple at, 166; *Weekly New Mexican* criticizes Army, 104, 127
Santa Fe Trail, 22
Santa Recia (Mexico), 171
Santa Rita Copper Mine, 29
Santa Rosa (Mexico), Apaches attack, 168
Scalp hunting, 11-15
Schaeffer, Charles M., 171, 174
Sheridan, Philip, 85, 92
Sherman, William T., 85, 102, 126, 162; commands Army, 37
Sibley, Henry H., Confederate commander in New Mexico, 29
Sierra Betanas Mountains (Mexico), 116
Sierra de Tosesigua (Mexico), 176
Sierra Negrita Range, Apaches found in, 121
Silver City (N.M.), 37, 151, 158; volunteers hunt Victorio, 137-38;

picture of, 138; citizens complain to President Hayes, 139; citizens organize, 142

Silver City Herald (N.M.), prints parts of Madden's diary, 137-38

Sioux Indians, 35

Sitting Bull, Sioux medicine man, 75

Slocum's Ranch (N.M.), Indians attack near, 102

Society, conflicts in, as contributor to Indian problems, 180

Socarro County (N.M.), 135; citizens complain about Army's inefficiency, 127

Soldier's Handbook, 55

Soledad Mountains (N.M.), 137

Sonoita River, 27

Sonoita Valley (Ariz.), 24

Sonora (Mexico), Indian raids in, 7

Spaniards: arrival in Southwest, 4, 5, 6; alliance with Apaches against Comanches, 6

Stoneman, George, commands Department of Arizona, 32

Sulphur Springs (Texas), 157

Tarahumara (Indian scouts), 176

Taylor, Zachary, 22

Terrazas, Joaquín, 75, 84, 85, 117, 146, 147, 169, 171, 172, 173, 174, 175, 176

Terrazas, Luis, Governor of Chihuahua, 17, 18, 19, 76, 117, 124, 146, 147, 153, 170, 171, 173

Territory of Arizona, Confederates organize, 27

Texas Rangers, 27, 111, 112, 116, 125, 126, 132, 146, 159, 160, 163, 170, 171, 174, 175; picture of, 125; search in Mexico, 161

Tiffany, J. C., Indian agent, 161

Tinaja de las Palmas, Grierson stops at, 153

Touey, Timothy, 130-31

Tres Castillos (Mexico), 176, 177, 178

Treviño, Geronimo, 117, 118, 119, 173; commands Mexican forces, 87

Trías, Angel, Governor of Chihuahua, 13, 16, 17, 18, 19, 104, 117, 118; offers reward for Kirker, 15

Tucson (Ariz.), 29, 94, 103; Indians attack, 32; citizens attack Camp Grant, 33; picture of, 103

Tularosa (N.M.) Mescalero Reservation, 41, 87, 89, 90, 124, 126, 128, 132, 133, 135, 136, 148, 151, 157, 162, 168-69; Victorio to be moved to, 86

Tularosa River, 40

Tunstall, John H., in Lincoln County War, 46

Tupper, Tullius C., searches for Apaches, 94

United States Army Manual, 58

United States Military Academy, 29, 34, 52, 61, 63, 75, 79, 92, 180; academic board, picture of, 52

Valle, Adolfo J., 147, 152, 153, 162, 173

Van Horn (Texas), 160; Grierson camps at, 155

Van Horn's Wells (Texas), 66

Varejo (N.M.), Indians attack, 102

Vicksburg (Miss.), Battle of, 61

Victorio, Apache chief, 4, 19, 39, 59, 71, 74, 75, 84, 85, 86, 87, 90, 92, 96, 99, 102, 104, 105-6, 107, 108, 111, 119, 122, 124, 126, 127, 128, 129, 130, 132, 133, 134, 136, 137, 142, 143, 144, 145, 147, 148, 149, 152, 153, 155, 157, 158, 159, 160, 161, 162, 163, 168, 170, 171, 176,

Victorio, Apache chief (*continued*)
177, 178, 179, 180, 183; scalp
bounty on, 11, reasons for refusal
to remain on reservation, 15;
wants separate reservation, 39;
local conditions as cause of hostilities, 44-47; birthplace and ancestry, 76-77; picture of, 77; flees
San Carlos, 79-81; influences
other Apaches to join, 88; followers declare they would fight until
death, 89; flees New Mexico reservation, 91; attacks Captain
Hooker, 94; false rumors of death,
98; falsely charged with raids,
103; Mexican government prepared to campaign against, 117; in
major fight against Carroll, 131;
reservation Indians ride with, 135;
raids near San Carlos, 139;
wounded in fight, 140; son killed
in fight, 145; Mescaleros help,
151; Texas Rangers chase, 174-
75; death, 176
Viele, Charles D., 154, 156

Walde, ———, stage driver, 159
Wallace, Lew, Governor of New
Mexico, 46, 91, 92, 102, 118,
119, 142-43

War of the Reform, 16
Ward, John, 24
Washington (Apache said to be
Victorio's son): leads raiders, 139;
killed, 145
Weatherford (Texas), 27
Webster, Daniel, Secretary of State,
23
Weekly New Mexican, gives realistic
appraisal of Hatch, 143
West, J. R., 30
West Point, *see* United States Mili-
tary Academy
Wichita Mountains (Indian Terri-
tory), 68
Wilcox, Orlando B., 119
Works of Sitting Bull, The, 75
Wright, Henry H., chases Apaches,
88
Wright, John T., 121

Yavapais Indians, surrender of, 35
Ysleta (Texas), 126; Baylor and
Rangers at, 113
Yuma Indians, 14, 15

Zimpleman Salt Lake (Texas), 160
Zuloaga, Juan, wagon train of, attacked, 121